D1595725

RACE—A CHRISTIAN SYMPOSIUM

RACE—A CHRISTIAN SYMPOSIUM

edited by

CLIFFORD S. HILL
&
DAVID MATHEWS

LONDON
VICTOR GOLLANCZ LTD
1968

575 00015 5

Printed in Great Britain by
The Camelot Press Ltd., London and Southampton

Biblical quotations throughout are taken from
the Revised Standard Version unless otherwise
stated.

FOREWORD

We welcome the appearance of this ecumenical symposium on race. This is a field in which Christians can speak with one voice and we are glad that such authoritative writers have combined to offer a significant contribution towards the elucidation of racial issues.

Conflicts between races are sad features of many modern societies. England may be more fortunate than some, but we are by no means free from difficulties. There are certainly people in Britain willing to exploit social problems and give them a racial slant.

Christians have to play their full part in creating a just society in the changing conditions in Britain. Every age has to think out afresh the principles of man's duty to man and the very importance of racial mixing in the present day makes it imperative that Christians apply to this task a mature understanding of the basis of human brotherhood.

We hope that this book will be widely read and discussed not only by Christians but by all men of goodwill.

Michael Cantuar : Archbishop of
Canterbury

+ John Card. Hssnard Cardinal Archbishop
of Westminster

Stew[anisch . Moderator of
Free Church
Federal Council

CONTENTS

RACE—A CHRISTIAN SYMPOSIUM

CHAPTER ONE

INTRODUCTORY

by

David Mathews, M.A.

Mr Mathews is director of Catholic Overseas
Appointments attached to the Catholic Institute
for International Relations. He was formerly a
District Commissioner in Tanganyika (Tanzania) and since his return to London has taken
an active part in the field of education in race
relations.

THE LITERATURE ON racial questions is already quite extensive and new books are being added each year. Many of these are concerned with a particular aspect of race or the special problems of one locality. What we have tried to do in this symposium is to examine the whole field of race from a Christian standpoint: an ambitious project in such a small book, but one surely worth attempting.

A number of Christian organizations in Britain have been active in the last few years in running conferences on racial questions and generally trying to awaken men's consciences. Church leaders, too, have made a number of pronouncements condemning the evils of prejudice and discrimination. We are beginning to see courses on race and immigration form part of the normal curriculum in colleges and seminaries. Gradually, teachers and youth workers and other educators are realizing that they need to be well-informed on these questions so that they can help others to reach a better understanding. It is not so much preaching that is required as educating in the widest sense. The enunciation of basic Christian principles, which still form the backbone of morality in this country, is only the first step; the implications of these principles have to be carefully studied. Their application to different concrete racial situations will then be easier, although wisdom and courage will still be required.

Our aim has been to restate in current terms the traditional Christian teaching on race and to attempt a clarification, within a Christian framework, of some of the fundamental issues involved. We think this symposium will be of use to all educators as a "source book" of authoritative Christian thinking. Such a book is certainly needed in this country.

It is interesting to see how, over the past decade, the attitudes of the opinion-formers in Britain have changed. The pattern used to be one of tolerance of the different races, but little more than that. As far as this country was concerned positive action was considered both unnecessary and unsuitable. There was opposition to any legislation whether to control the number of immigrants coming into the country or to secure special services or fair treatment for them on arrival. Nowadays we find an intense concern on the part of these same opinion-formers and a willingness to try any measures which may help to build a just society. Tolerance is not enough.

In part, of course, this change is simply a result of the changed situation—the large number of immigrants and the obvious permanence of their stay. But partly it is the realization that Britain, in practice and certainly in potential, has as much racial prejudice and discrimination as any other country. For anybody even moderately well informed it would seem impossible to deny the existence of widespread discrimination based on colour. The Political and Economical Planning 1967 report on Racial Discrimination provides all-too-solid evidence of this injustice; organizations like the Campaign Against Racial Discrimination have brought a number of particular instances to light. For anyone who has tried to work in the field of race relations this evidence was hardly necessary.

How often the view can be heard expressed—at meetings of reponsible Christians—that the problem is not really a racial one but social or "economic". All would be well in time, they say, if people were left alone and given a chance to settle down. The speakers do not see that their attitudes are seriously at fault; that they have to rethink all their old assumptions in the light of the new multi-racial situation. People who talk like this are refusing to recognize the nature and size of the problem, and the fact that it has yet to reach its peak with the rapid coming-of-age of the immigrants' children. Such apathy does much to increase racial bitterness. People are evidently able to deplore prejudice without perceiving that they are one of its causes. There is much work yet to be done in Britain in awakening men's consciences on questions of race and colour.

All men have consciences and the word is not being used here in any specifically Christian sense. No one can shed responsibility for his conduct towards other members of society. Nevertheless it is tempting for a Christian to hope for a more enlightened attitude on the part of fellow Christians in this country. After all, the pronouncements from the churches, at any rate at the top, have become very forceful in the last few years: condemnation of hatred and injustice between races has been explicit. Nor is the New Testament any less clear in saying what our duty should be towards our fellow men. Yet the bulk of Christians in Britain behave no differently from anyone else.

This book is not the place to publish the results of research done by such bodies as the Catholic Institute for International Relations. Washing dirty linen in public is an exercise of limited value and in any case no one really believes that Christians are less prejudiced or less ignorant than anybody else. Why bother to prove it? Nevertheless, it did seem appropriate to include three brief essays by "coloured" people living in Britain, as these in themselves could serve as a sufficient indictment of the Christian population. The writers give a very different picture of the British scene from that of some complacent Englishmen and I think they may be fairly described as typical view-points. Writing as Christians, all three make it clear that in this crucial period of race relations in Britain, Christians as a whole have not given the lead that they hoped to see.

It may be felt that there is no need for a specifically Christian approach to race relations, which is a secular subject (apart from particular pastoral problems). Certainly many others share the views of Christians in these matters, particularly in Britain with its strong Christian heritage. Christians are glad to find others thinking the same as they do; they see no merit merely in being different. But in this, as in other fundamental questions of human relations, Christian morality, or more particularly the Christian view of what man is, should give a coherent and recognizable picture. It should provide special insights which can be grasped and developed by Christians and non-Christians alike. Happily this is a field where Christians of all persuasions can co-operate; in the preparation of this symposium denominational differences have not intruded at all.

This is not to suggest that on any particular issue there is only one Christian answer. We know that Christians disagree with each other on a number of questions: for example, the extent to which the State should interfere in preventing racial discrimination. The application of the Christian view of life to particular situations is never easy and different conclusions are possible. The attempt, however, must be made in everyday life. It is no good taking refuge in social or family complications as a way of avoiding full Christian commitment. When properly grasped, the principles which come through in this book should be able to illuminate the most humdrum racial situation, whether in Britain or elsewhere.

Christians, both as individuals and as Churches, have a lead to give. They must make sure that the Christian view of race, which is really one aspect of the Christian view of man, is known and understood by themselves and by other Christians; then they most make this vision clear to be appraised and considered by those who are not of the Christian faith.

In this symposium we have tried to cover all the main fields of study connected with race: migration in its different aspects; psychological and sociological forces; the biology of race and inter-marriage; race in the Bible and current Christian teaching. The short chapter called "A Look at Britain" has been included as a reminder of the realities of a one racial situation, to present in particular the world being discussed in general terms in the more scholarly chapters.

We have been fortunate in obtaining contributions from men and women who are really eminent in their own fields of study. They are indeed all Christians and have had to make the attempt to integrate the teachings of Christ with their own view of the world. It is, however, as recognized authorities that they have been asked to contribute and it as such that they deserve to be read. Because of its emotional overtones, race is a subject on which clear and informed thinking is essential; our contributors, authorities who are also Christians, have been asked for just this. Each, of course, is expressing his own opinion.

So often in discussing the racial situation in Britain or elsewhere an intensely pessimistic note is struck. When viewing the progress made so far it is all too easy to be despondent. But surely, provided a man is prepared to take an honest look at his human situation and to renounce the purely selfish approach, the Christian vision of man must sound a note of optimism.

> "Christianity is certainly not melancholy, it is, on the contrary, glad tidings—for the melancholy; to the frivolous it is certainly not glad tidings, for it wishes first of all to make them serious." (Kierkegaard: *Journals* (1847)—Fontana Edition, p. 129)

The aim of this book is to help people to think seriously about relations between races. It is to help people adopt a responsible attitude to one of the world's most pressing problems and, for Christians, one of their greatest challenges. In attempting this we realize that there is a limit to what teaching and preaching and legislating can achieve. Ultimately, "good race relations" is not something that can be taught. Like all other aspects of living with his fellow men it is something that each individual has to struggle with and realise in his own everyday life.

CHAPTER TWO

MIGRATION IN A WORLD SETTING

by

Philip Mason, M.A., C.I.E., O.B.E.

Mr Mason is Director of the Institute of Race
Relations, and was formerly Director of Studies
in Race Relations at the Royal Institute of
International Affairs. When in the Indian
Civil Service he wrote under the pseudonym
of Philip Woodruff.

Early Movements of Man

Man—a creature that uses fire and tools and has a sense of the divine—is the most widespread and adaptable of mammalian species. In his earliest stages, he was a gatherer of food, not anchored to a territory by cultivation. And there is good evidence that he migrated constantly, in search of better food and conditions, not only between a winter territory and a summer territory and such other seasonal movement, but across whole continents. Consider for instance the widely accepted hypothesis that the American Indians came from Asia across the Bering Strait and moved southwards right down to the tip of South America.

This is not to suggest that migration came to an end with agriculture. The American Indians were cultivating maize at an early stage of their immense journey; many other vast migrations were made by cultivating peoples—the Bantu-speaking peoples of Africa southwards, the Sanskrit-speakers eastwards into India, and people with a related language southward into Greece. It would be easy to go on giving examples. But what concerns us is the results of these migrations. They were very various; sometimes the migrants found peoples more primitive than themselves in their way and enslaved them as the Dorians did with the Helots in the Peloponnese; sometimes barbarian hordes overthrew a more advanced civilization, as the Goths did Rome; rather differently, the Manchus, a much less developed people, conquered and ruled China but accepted its civilization.

It is hard to think of peoples at different stages of development who seem to have fused quickly and easily. At a primitive stage, the men of the defeated party were sometimes killed and the women taken as prizes; the culture of the winning party would then usually prevail. The book of Judges in the Old Testament is a detailed early record of a piecemeal, rather haphazard, conquest of a settled people by puritanical nomads from the desert. They seem to have moved step by step; they often lived by the side of Canaanitish peoples. It seems likely that this account is historically much nearer accuracy than that in the book of Joshua which describes a complete planned conquest and extermination of the defeated. Much of the Old Testament is concerned with the tendency of the Israelites to "whore after strange gods", which they would hardly have done if the Canaanites had been destroyed as completely as the later editions of Joshua would have us think.

But if complete extermination was rarer than is sometimes suggested, it is possible to say that in early migrations one of two peoples who met usually disappeared in the end as a separate entity. Sometimes the conquerors imposed themselves as an aristocracy and in the course of time melted into the majority, like the Normans in England—though not before they had profoundly influenced the culture of the defeated. Sometimes it was the defeated who disappeared as a separate folk, like the Romanized British before the Saxons in the greater part of England. Biologically, one can hardly doubt that their genes survived; invaders who came in ships would be short of women. It was their culture that disappeared. But it is worth noting that some peoples seem to have made a conscious decision not to mix with those they had defeated; the Spartans kept themselves completely aloof from the indigenous Helots, and the Aryan invaders of India—probably elaborating on something they found in existence—built up the elaborate social device of caste for keeping groups of people apart and a mythology, with no doubt an element of truth in it, that the higher castes were the descendants of invaders. But this postponement of fusion produces far more acute crisis in the end.

European Migrations

We have been looking at migrations which took place on foot or with simple means of navigation. With the expansion of European peoples at the end of the fifteenth century to America, Asia, Africa, Australia, a new phase opens in the story. But it is not, at first, so markedly different. The passions of mankind have not changed within recorded history. People migrate for reasons they may not always know themselves. They are usually searching for food or wealth; they look for a land flowing with milk and honey even when they are also inspired by an idea, such as the conversion or slaughter of the heathen. The invasion of Canaan by the Jews, the Islamic conquest of North Africa and Spain, the Spanish conquest of Mexico and Peru—no one can say that the economic motive was absent.

On the other hand, who can be sure that it would have been enough without religious conviction too? Some people stay for generations where their ancestors lived, though they might be better fed somewhere else; they lack the spark that might fire them to look behind the ranges. Even the migration of Irish and central Europeans to Canada and the United States in the nineteenth century was not wholly economic; there was usually a political, sometimes a religious, element too, a search for freedom as well as food. To South Africa and New Zealand, migrants went to seek adventure as well as to seek a fortune.

The European migrations then, like those that came before, arose from mixed motives and they produced even more mixed results. In Tasmania, a deliberate attempt was made to exterminate the natives by poison; in North America it was a common saying that the only good Indian was a dead Indian. In Mexico, in the course of 400 years, there has been much mixture of Spanish and Amerindian blood and some mixture of cultures, some fusing of religious ideas, at least in the popular mind; in South Africa, the Spartan and Indian device of a rigidly separate Helot race has been adopted.

Compulsory Migration

All this was voluntary migration. But there was compulsory migration, too, of convicts as indentured servants to the West Indies and America and to Australia. Much more far-reaching in its consequences was the slave trade, from Africa westward to North and South America and to the Caribbean, eastward to Arabia and Asia Minor. The Africans transported to the New World usually suffered a fate worse than the Israelites in Babylon, because people of different languages and customs were mixed and herded together like animals in the slave plantations;

they lost language, religion, family ties, custom—all the heritage built up by man over the ages. The whole world still suffers for that wrong.

Economic Motives

Motives—I have already suggested—are seldom wholly economic. But a century and more ago, it was a dogma that "economic man" pursued aims purely economic and that the "laws of political economy" worked in the long run for the general good, provided governments did not interfere. Wealth, goods, labour, flowed to where they were needed; men would go from poor countries with high population density to richer countries in need of labour just as inevitably as the wind blows from an area of high pressure to one of low. But of course man is much more complex in his needs and behaviour than barometric pressure; people are not just labour, and they did not move like this in the nineteenth century.

India was a poor country, already very densely populated a century ago, but there was no movement to Britain, an industrialized country, then the richest and most advanced in the world. The weight of custom has to be taken into account; the idea of migration has to spread. At that time it was a British assumption that Britain, as a free country, was a political refuge open to anyone, from anywhere in the world, a home to any British subject in the Empire; it was another British assumption that while Indian rajahs and students might come here, Indian manual workers would never dream of coming to Britain to earn their living. In fact they did not.

The "laws of political economy" operated greatly to our advantage in respect of capital and goods; we lent capital and received interest; we imported raw materials and exported manufactures to half the world, with, at this stage, very little competition. As to people, there was a kind of built-in but invisible valve that regulated the flow also to our advantage; on the whole they went out poor and came back rich.

Modern Population Movements

By the 1950's, all this was changed. In the case of the Caribbean, other outlets for emigrants, notably the United States, had
been closed. But in general, it was almost equally important
that there was a change in men's minds. Ideas of independence,
of human equality, had become widespread. At the same time,
a new dimension had been added to migration. Travel by air is
now much quicker and little more expensive than by sea and
the separation from home and friends seems far less final. To go
from England to Australia once meant a separation that would
probably last a lifetime; in the 1950's, the journey from Jamaica
to England could be accomplished in a few hours and was more
like a voyage across the Irish Sea had once been.

The migration of conquest seems now a thing of the past; the
migrant goes not in order to rule—as Romans went to Palestine,
Spaniards to Peru, English to India—but as a suppliant in the
first place, with the aim of making a better living than he could
at home, perhaps eventually of becoming a citizen of a new
country. In Britain, a flow of such migrants began in the 1950's,
first from the Caribbean, later from India and Pakistan. There
was no legal bar to the entry of Commonwealth citizens.

There has always been a conflict between British ideals and
our attitude in practice. We have pictured ourselves as a
political asylum for oppressed foreigners, a mother to the
Empire, but in practice we are a society divided into small and
self-contained units, jealous of strangers, wary of committing
ourselves to relationships that make new demands. We can in
time absorb small numbers of immigrants; since 1945, we have,
with many difficulties but some success, absorbed Italians, Poles,
Hungarians. These, however, were foreign subjects and since
1914, aliens have been controlled by strict regulations. They
must report to the police at regular intervals and at least until
they are accepted as naturalized citizens they must continually
renew their permit to stay in the country. But once they are
naturalized, these legal restrictions disappear and, though an
unusual accent may distinguish the first generation, their

children will be indistinguishable from the children of the native-born.

This was not true of the children of the West Indians or Indo-Pakistanis. They are distinguished by colour and, in the case of Indians and Pakistanis, by religion, language and culture. Colour is a visible sign of this which will persist in later generations, and it presents us with a sharp national challenge. It brings the conflict between ideals and behaviour to a far severer point than Poles or Hungarians ever did. It exposes also a contradiction in our attitude to the Commonwealth; we have professed to be part of a multi-racial Commonwealth in which all are equal, but in practice most of us think of the old or white Dominions as quite different in status from the nations who have become independent since the Second World War.

Restrictions on Immigration

I have tried to suggest that in the nineteenth century and early part of this century there was a kind of one-way valve as regards migration, and it did not really occur to any but a very small number of West Indians or Indians to come to this country and settle. When this one-way valve was removed in the 1950's the flow began to increase and, as everybody knows, the Commonwealth Immigrants Act 1962 was introduced, which limits the numbers permitted to come in. Further limitations have since been added to those under the original Act. The arguments about the Act are complex, and demand not a short article, but quite a long book. But let us look at them briefly.

There are first various arguments which are based purely on national selfishness. They are far from being unanimous or clear. There are some people who maintain that if we had rigidly excluded unskilled immigrants from say 1952 onwards, the shortage of labour in the country would have been so great that by now we should have been everywhere forced to introduce automation and would have had to make so much better use of our existing manpower as greatly to improve our economy and increase our wealth. Others say that an expanding economy needs a rapidly expanding labour force and that internal markets are a means by which external are developed; they point to examples of the United States and of West Germany, who have expanded their labour force and their internal markets and have continued to flourish as a result.

Whatever the upshot of this economic argument—and it has not yet received the detailed treatment it needs—the real reason for the Commonwealth Immigrants Act and the subsequent tightening of the regulations is not purely economic, but is the result of fears—mainly cultural—and of the political consequences of that fear. People are frightened of large numbers of those who seem to be different. They say that their fear has to do with houses and jobs, but there is also a deeper fear of cultural change. They do not want to find themselves in the middle of a society which is predominantly Hindu or Muslim or West Indian. These fears, whether we think they are rational or not, were strongly expressed at the time of the election in 1964. They were reported from all over the country and in a democracy were bound to produce political reaction.

Many people were shocked and horrified by the illiberal and unChristian nature of these fears and the political consequences of them in increased restrictions on the entry of immigrants. They argue that the flow of migration was comparatively slight before the idea of the Commonwealth Immigrants Act was introduced and that the great increase in numbers in the last year before it came into force was largely due to a rush to "beat the ban". This, however, is only partly true. The rush to beat the ban did take place, but the old mental one-way valve had been removed and there was already an organized business in selling passages on aircraft to people from certain parts of India and Pakistan as well as from the Caribbean. There is little doubt that without the Commonwealth Immigrants Act the numbers would have increased steadily as they had been doing during the period before the "beat the ban" rush began. This whole question introduces a dilemma which is of real concern to Christians who try to look at the world in a realistic kind of way.

I do not propose here to argue the general question of race,

but it is worth remembering that the scientific investigations
which have so far been undertaken seem to indicate that environment and upbringing are of major importance in the development of any individual person, and that individuals of more
than average, or less than average, ability seem to occur about
as often in one race as in another. Of course the results of
environment have meant that the achievements of some races
has been far greater than that of others.

It is one of the basic assumptions of Christians that every
human being has some potential of development and that it is
the duty of others to try to help that potential to be realized and
not to hamper it. On these grounds anyone who professes to be
a Christian must feel it to be wrong that one section of mankind
should barricade itself off into an area of greater opportunity to
which it denies entry to others. A population which has access
to fertile lands, developed institutions and a high standard of
living has a better chance of leisure and thought and worship.

But against this general consideration, which is widespread
among people of good will, must be set another Christian duty.
This is to face the fact that human beings are not perfect nor
perfectible; to insist that they are is to fall into the old heresy of
Pelagius. They are insecure and subject above all to fear, and
under the influence of fear behave to each other like devils. We
have to put some trust in human nature, but surely it is right
and prudent to order our affairs in such a way that we do not
strain probabilities too far. It is surely right, for instance, for a
Government to take steps to prevent the meeting of a group of
nuclear disarmers with a group of British Fascists, or of Ulster
Orangemen with a Catholic procession, or—looking back to my
own experience—a Hindu procession passing a Mosque at mid-
day on Friday.

On these grounds it seems to me inevitable that a government
—so long as we have national governments responsible to
national popular opinion, a point to which I shall return—
should accept the necessity of some limitation on the flow of an
agricultural population from over-populated and poor countries
such as India with a national income of less than £30 a year to

an industrialized country such as Britain with an income of rather more like £400 per person. If there is free entry, the economic incentive is bound in the long run to bring more and more, and as their numbers are so much greater than those in this island, there is a real likelihood of cultural change which people fear and which they will resist violently if the threat is too sudden and too sharp for them to face.

The Need for International Agreement

On the other hand, to deny entry altogether would clearly be wrong, being essentially selfish and—to appeal to a wider audience—in the long run foolishly selfish. Do we really want to see a world in which the rich white nations have shut themselves into an enclosed fold in which they get richer and richer, keeping out the poor nations altogether? The fact that there is this difference of colour and that the white nations on the whole are in the rich group—the only really significant exception being Japan—adds an extra bitterness to the hostility that is likely to result from such a situation; there are already plenty of signs of this world hostility.

It is true that the poor nations are far from united, but there are certain issues on which they can be counted on to be unanimous and one of them is race. And, still for the moment looking at this from a purely selfish point of view, we are faced with the frightful dilemma that the only secular hope for our future in a nuclear world lies in the development of some supranational force, some form of international agreement which would approach in the end to a world government, which will control the use of military nuclear weapons. And yet the whole future of such an organization is bedevilled by the jealousy and hostility that results from the feeling of most of the non-white peoples that the white peoples have been selfish in the past and have exploited them commercially and, what is worst of all, still regard them with contempt.

This is a world dilemma, I would almost say *the* world dilemma. Every act of intolerance to others in Britain and America makes it worse.

B

This is not an argument for opening the doors to unlimited immigration, because the likelihood is that this would produce elections in which race would be an issue, resulting in race riots much more serious than those of Notting Hill in 1959 and similar manifestations. This is an argument for a double policy, of a controlled flow of immigrants and for a liberal policy to those who are already here. By liberal is meant something a good deal warmer than just letting them find their own level. It means a positive attempt to help them to fit into British society.

This does not imply that they should become entirely indistinguishable from native Englishmen, that they should give up eating curry and rice and take to fish and chips. It means that the efforts of the Government should be directed to achieving a kind of society in which there is cultural tolerance and religious tolerance; a warm, positive tolerance directed to understanding and accepting national differences, but in which there should be a genuine equality of opportunity in education, jobs, housing and public places.

The Implications

There are two serious implications to this, implications with very far-reaching consequences. It is probable that a sub-conscious fear of these consequences worries many people and induces the fear to which I have referred. It is rational to find them worrying, but they must be faced. The first is that we live in a world in which the cities, the great urban centres and conurbations, are the centre of industry, of decision and of national life. In these cities, life is bound to be less tightly-knit into homogeneous local groups than it has been in the past. If they are ever to become healthy and happy places in which men can live, they will have to consist of a great variety of groups of people. They are likely to be international and cosmopolitan in the sense that there will be groups from many different countries of origin, from many religions and races. The object at which we should aim is that these groups should be overlapping and not mutually exclusive, that their members should also belong to other groups who are interested in various skills or forms of entertainment or forms of leisure and recreation which bring them together. This means an end to the culturally homogeneous nation.

The other great consequence of what I have been saying has already been hinted at. It is that not only has the day of national homogeneity passed, but the day of national sovereignty is really over. We ought, both as prudent people and as Christians, to be looking forward to the day when national sovereignty will step by step be handed over to a world government.

Both of these consequences are to most English people somewhat alarming. We have lived in far greater security in the past than the rest of the world, and we have developed many national ways and characteristics which we are reluctant to lose. Yet there is no doubt that we ought to face the "diminishment", as Teilhard de Chardin would call it, involved in these steps. But it is a diminishment only in his special sense. We have also to recognize that variety means life and richness and a multiplicity of invention, while a monochrome uniformity means a dearth of all these things, and particularly of invention, imagination and of originality. It could be argued, though there is clearly no room for it in this chapter, that human progress has been almost always the result of a mixing or a meeting of cultures.

CHAPTER THREE

THE RIGHTS OF INDIVIDUALS AND DUTIES OF STATES

by

Tadeusz Stark, LL.D.

Dr Stark, an international jurist, is Secretary
General of the International Catholic Migration
Commission, Geneva, which has consultative
status with the United Nations, U.N.I.C.E.F.,
and the Council of Europe.

Natural and Positive Rights

Jurisprudence defines "the right" as a claim to have or to do something, the justice and equity of which are determined by some law, i.e. by a legal norm.

It usually distinguishes between the *natural* right and the *positive* right. The first is constituted by the natural reasoning of human beings, called human conscience, which tells us what a person's free action should be in conformity with his reasonable nature. The second, the positive right, is established by a particular legislative body and is included in legislation.

The natural right is immutable and binds all human consciences, because the Creator has endowed all human beings with it, whereas the positive right can be revoked and changed. But at the same time, the natural right may evolve in so far as the conscience of man or of nations comes to know the requirements of justice more clearly.

The cataclysm of the last World War has shown plainly that positive rights do not suffice, because very often State absolutism, based on the doctrine of nation and race, denies the value and dignity of man and is diametrically opposed to natural rights. The nation and race in totalitarian systems are considered to be absolute and man is held for nothing.

The effective protection of the individual today requires a reconsideration of the principles on which the present legal order reposes. The rethinking of legal principles has given birth to many efforts to codify and define "human rights" in various declarations and charters, of which the Universal Declaration of the United Nations, proclaimed in 1948, is the climax.

The Universal Declaration of Human Rights

The meaning of the Universal Declaration lies in the idea that man as a member of the human race has some rights which must be respected beyond national borders. This "internationalization" is founded on the assumption that the national protection of rights does not suffice and that international guarantees are needed. Besides, the international character of the Declaration is reflected in formulating rights that no national law has been able to lay down, as they go beyond the boundaries of a country. For instance, article 6 foresees that "everyone has the right to recognition *everywhere* as a person before the law". In article 15 we find the right of *everyone* to a nationality (no national authority can decree that every human being has the right to be incorporated in a nation). Likewise, in article 14, the Declaration refers to the right of *everyone* to be protected against persecution, by seeking and enjoying asylum in *other* countries.

The Universal Declaration does not, however, constitute a juridical document in the sense of positive law, but only "a common standard of achievement for all peoples and all nations" that every individual and every organ of society, should keep constantly in mind and consequently "strive by teaching and education to promote respect for these rights and freedoms and to secure their universal and effective recognition and observance."

It is of some interest to juxtapose the Universal Declaration of Human Rights with the encyclical of the late Pope John XXIII *Pacem in Terris* proclaimed in 1963. *Pacem in Terris* contains the most complete declaration of human rights ever written by a pope. It also refers directly to the Universal Declaration which is presented as "a step towards the establishment of a juridico-political organization of the world community". With this encyclical, the Catholic Church gave its full approval to the Declaration of Human Rights. There is a close relationship between the two documents, some passages of the encyclical literally reproducing the text of the Universal Declaration (for instance article 25 on social security).

Freedom of Movement

It is not easy to define the spheres of activity of the State and the individual where migration is concerned. Migration is considered a basic and primary right because there is hardly anything which restricts the activity of a person more than limitations on his freedom of movement. It is difficult to imagine that with all our modern methods of travel, many people are still compelled to stay at home. Nor is the loss only theirs: the violation of this fundamental right involves a loss of freedom on the part of humanity in general, since migration is an important factor in the progress of civilization.

The right to migrate may be defined as a right to leave or to enter permanently any territory, especially a national one. One also speaks of the right to free movement. The science of law usually distinguishes between the *right to emigrate* which is the right of everyone to leave any country, especially his own national country, and the *right to immigrate*, e.g. the right to enter a chosen country in order to settle permanently and to work there. Some theoreticians also speak of the right to re-emigrate, when it is a question of returnee movements between countries or of second migration movements. To stress the political aspect of forcible migration, some lawyers also speak of the *right to seek refuge* and the *right to grant asylum* which correspond to the freedom of a political refugee to emigrate and to immigrate.

Migration was at one time the purely private matter of the individuals concerned and people were less willing to leave their own country to migrate. Nowadays, in view of the efficient means of communication available, individuals and groups cross frontiers much more easily. At one time the receiving countries did not contest the validity of this right because of their need for manpower. But from the end of the nineteenth century there has been a marked change of attitude. Today there are restrictions in force both in the sending countries which do not wish to lose their people and in the receiving countries which arbitrarily protect their own citizens.

The Christian position in this domain is to grant freedom to migrate while at the same time respecting the rights of other people or countries.

Catholic social doctrine considers the right of migration as a *restricted natural right*. It is a "natural right" because it flows from nature, not from a society. Thus it is not merely a positive right granted by the State. But it is a derived natural right subject to certain limitations vested in the States which must also be respected. The general teaching of the Church can be summarized in the following way:

(1) The right of migration is not established or determined by a State or by a community of States, but it is a natural heritage and natural right of man which cannot be denied or nullified by acts of governments.

(2) Families have the inalienable and natural right to find living space through freedom to migrate, especially when they live in overpopulated countries and a more favourable distribution of people and access to natural resources can be found.

(3) Modern conditions make the reasonable regulation of emigration and immigration legitimate, but the power of the State to regulate this right may only be exercised for adequate, just and proportionally grave reasons based on objectively sound moral considerations and the notion of "common good" both for emigration and immigration.

(4) Previous orientation and training of migrants, planned settlements and economic integration and the conclusion between nations of mutual migration agreements are desirable; they should be prepared and supervised by national and international migration organizations throughout the world.

Can we say that these principles are observed by modern States? If we look at the various pieces of legislation in force, the result will often be disappointing. In many countries, the natural right of men to migrate is so restricted by law that injustice is done to people in need. Some States have also misinterpreted the principle of regulating migration and have made unnecessary and arbitrary restrictions and have imposed quotas. There are too many overpopulated areas in the world which could be relieved by a more favourable distribution of the population and too many "lands without people" which could

accept new inhabitants. Finally, the organization of international migration leaves much to be desired and the preparation of migrants is not carried out properly.

Emigration

The right of emigration at a *national* level is seldom recognized in constitutions and fundamental laws, and hardly any
State admits that discrimination plays any part whatsoever in
its determination of an individual's right to leave the country.
In fact, there are at present a number of people who are not
permitted to emigrate as a result of a generally applied policy
referred to as national security, public order or public health.
The concept of the "national security" is, however, so broad
that it may very often be invoked to cover a whole variety of
other motives, when, in fact, no question of national security is
involved. Moreover, certain States which fully recognize the
right of emigration permit wide administrative discretion in
determining whether or not a particular departure is against
the interests of the State. There are also indirect ways of preventing a person from leaving: for instance, the State may put
severe restrictions upon the amount of personal property an
emigrant is allowed to take out of the country and in practice,
this amounts to a negation of the right to leave the country.
Refusal to grant a passport to a citizen is another example of
indirect discrimination by the State against the individual. A
general prohibition of religious pilgrimages or meetings involv-
ing travel abroad is also a serious limitation of freedom of
movement.

For these reasons, it has long been felt that the right to emigrate should be guaranteed at an *international* level.

The Code of International Ethics supports the right of the
individual to emigrate, in the following words:

> "Man cannot live outside the bounds of all society, but he is
> not so chained to the land of his birth or to the territory
> whence he comes that he cannot break these bonds and start
> afresh in another social organism. As the master of his own

destiny, he has the right to "go forth from his country and from his kindred, and from his father's house" (Genesis xii. 1) and to seek under other skies and in foreign nations the means of realizing the end for which he was created."

After the Second World War, the United Nations established two legal prescriptions in this respect:

(1) **Paragraph 2 of article 13** of the Universal Declaration of Human Rights, and

(2) **Article 12** of the Covenant on Civil and Political Rights.

Article 13, paragraph 2 reads as follows: "Everyone has the right to leave any country, including his own, and to return to his country." Thus it joins two aspects together: emigration and re-migration.

Article 12 of the Covenant is more explicit. It provides: (*a*) that the right to leave a country "shall not be subject to any restrictions except those which are provided by law, are necessary to protect national security, public order, public health or morals, or the rights and freedoms of others, and are consistent with other rights recognized in this Covenant"; and (*b*) that "no one shall be arbitrarily deprived of the right to enter his own country."

In the light of the discussions of the United Nations Commission on Human Rights and its Sub-Commissions since 1954, a tentative proposal was submitted in 1961, but so far it has not been voted and accepted. We may therefore try to define some Christian principles which should guide the States in dealing with emigration.

Christian social doctrine recognizes the right of the individual (whether national citizen or foreigner) to leave any country. This recognition is the logical consequence of the relations between the human being and society, because the former should enjoy certain rights which are prior to society and which society must guarantee. On the other hand, the person is subordinate to the "common good" of society; but by its laws, the State should not do violence to anything that pertains to human nature. Even social values are a function of the person. In the light of the supreme value of the human being, the State may only forbid emigration for "valid reasons".

Emigration can also be seen as the greatest means of giving the family a chance to acquire property and sufficient living space. As is emphasised in *Rerum Novarum*, no private property is more in conformity with nature than land.

What then are the limits of the State's powers in this respect?

First, the State should never pass any measure which may, directly or indirectly, deprive any individual of the opportunity to leave a country on such grounds as race, colour, sex, language, religion, contrary political opinions, national or social origin, property, birth or other status.

The individual should be subject to restrictions only if they are provided by law and have a protective character with regard to national security, public order, public health or morals, or to possible infringement of the rights of others.

If the reason of national security is invoked, it should be clearly stated, except in the case of compelling reasons as when their disclosure would reveal State secrets or be prejudicial to friendly relations with other States. Limitations of a protective character may be invoked for reasons of health in the case of infectious diseases or epidemics and of morals for criminals or debtors.

The limitation of emigration for the economic interests of the State or for the expansion of various spheres of national activity is sometimes quoted as permissible. It may, in fact, happen that the State has a valid reason for preventing emigration when economic resources are available on the spot or the needs of production require it. But to have legitimate reasons for forbidding emigration, it is not enough for there to be sufficient resources for use over a long period of time; it is necessary for these resources to offer sufficient work and living conditions to all.

The requirement of a passport (for a citizen) or of an exit visa (for a foreigner) should be limited to a minimum or abolished entirely on the basis of bilateral or multi-lateral agreements.

When the required travel documents are refused, the applicant should be informed of the decision within a reasonable period of time and he should be given the right of appeal to a higher administrative level or to a court of law.

Currency or other financial controls should not be used by the State as a pretext for impeding the right of emigration and excessive taxes should not be imposed on travel documents. In the same spirit, deposits or any other type of security required to ensure the repatriation of the individual or to prevent him from becoming a public charge abroad should never be set so high as to constitute a virtual denial of permission to emigrate.

The majority of recommendations mentioned above were the objects of discussions and reports at an international level, but they have not yet been considered as legally binding on any State. They were also the object of a statement made by the International Catholic Migration Commission at the 19th Session of the Commission of Human Rights in March, 1963, where several principles were pointed out, namely that the violation of the right to emigrate infringes on other basic rights such as to found families, to associate with relatives or to practice religion, and that an effective remedy against arbitrary action by a Government would be the right of an aggrieved person to bring his case before an independent or impartial body.

Immigration

Unlike the existing right of emigration, there is no general recognition at the international level, of the right to immigrate. In fact, no provision for it appears in the Universal Declaration of Human Rights or any other United Nations Covenant. The problem confronting the States involved is the following: has an unexploited or rich country the right to prohibit the entry of immigrants because its own people should be the first to benefit from their country's wealth? Has a man the right to move freely to the areas of the earth where he may better employ his talents? If so, is such a right an absolute right or are there any considerations which should restrain this right?

The churches have often proclaimed the duty of nations to receive immigrants, but it has become clear that there is no question of an unrestricted absolute right, either for the migrant or for the receiving country. When speaking to the Senators of the United States in 1946, Pius XII openly stressed: "It is not surprising that changing circumstances have brought about a certain *restriction* being placed on foreign immigration; for in this matter not only the interests of the immigrant, but the welfare of the country must also be consulted." In 1947 he repeated: "The question of immigration today presents wholly new problems. As always, the welfare of the country must be considered, as well as the interests of the individual seeking entrance, and in the nature of things, circumstances will at times dictate a law of restriction. But by the same token, circumstances at times will almost cry out for an easing of the application of the law." And the explicit reason for this was given in 1948: "If in some locality, the land offers the possibility of supporting a large number of people, the sovereignty of the State cannot be exaggerated to the point that access to this land is, for inadequate or unjustified reasons, denied to needy and decent people from other nations, whenever this does not hinder the public welfare considered objectively." In 1950, he expressly stressed the rights of families: "It is necessary to face with all its implications the duty of providing innumerable facilities in their natural, moral, legal and economic unity, a just living space fulfilling sufficiently the requirements of human dignity."

Against this background we can analyse what limitations on immigration it is reasonable for States to impose.

An outstanding contribution to the problem of the right of immigration was made in 1961 by the World Council of Churches at its conference in Leysin. Professor Colin W. Williams' report analysing the Australian immigration policy, ended with the conclusion that:

"the State has the right to restrict immigration of foreigners to the extent necessary to keep the level of order and stability necessary to maintain justice and peace and to meet the human needs of its people. These policies, however, must be seen as "provisional" and must be flexible and progressive, moving towards that ultimate community where all discrimination on the basis of race, culture, ability, wealth and health are broken down."

Professor Williams clearly pointed out the opposition of the Australian Council of Churches to policies which are based on (*a*) national discrimination, as they conflict with God's desire to overcome it, (*b*) requirements that those desiring to enter should contribute economically to the new country and should be in good health, as this requirement contradicts the moral responsibility of every country to accept a fair share of the "hard core" people, and (*c*) requirements that care must be taken to accept only those whose cultural background is such as to create the minimum of cultural conflict, because cultural isolation cuts across God's purpose of gathering all men in Christ. In view of the State's tendencies to consider only economic interests, the author stressed the necessity for a government to move with all reasonable speed towards the creation of a community with the maximum openness consistent with economic stability and to overcome the prejudices which lie at the root of cultural conflicts. The State should see the wider human needs beyond national borders.

The Rights of Immigrants

It will be clear that neither the individual nor the State has an absolute right to either ask for admittance or to forbid immigration. No State possesses political or economic sovereignty absolutely as if it alone existed. The domination of a sovereign State over its territory is limited by the international community in the same way as the owner of private property within the State. Having available resources, the State cannot close its frontiers to immigrants, and any arbitrary limitation as regards both the number and the kind of immigrants is unjust. In its own interests the State can establish limitations only if it maintains the principle of common good and co-operates in solving the problems of other countries. If the State legislates quotas, they will only be legitimate if they are inspired by socio-economic motives and seek to avoid undue competition and conflicts between the native labour and the newcomers. If the reasons for these conflicts disappear, the quotas should be abolished. The qualitative limitation of immigrants is also just if it is based on protection against disease, criminals or morally suspect persons. The State may also select the labour force suitable for the country, in view of the necessity to co-ordinate immigration with economic programmes.

Once the immigrants are admitted, they cannot claim an absolute right to housing or to work. As far as social and economic claims are concerned the State is only obliged to grant immigrants equal treatment with the native citizens. Political equality will have to be achieved gradually, with due regard to the cultural assimilation of the immigrants.

In the preceding pages efforts have been made to lay down a broad outline of the Christian approach to the problem of human rights and especially the right of migration. It will be apparent that in spite of the principles of natural law, the clear teachings of the Church and the numerous writings of Christian philosophers, the regulation of human rights on an international level is still very imperfect. It becomes a particularly difficult task if racial conflict is involved.

However, only a moral solution is valid in this respect and it should be based on two principles: the dignity of man and the brotherhood of man. Discrimination in human rights, apart from the individual injustices it occasions, is morally untenable, because it denies this dignity of man and the unity of the human race established by the Creator.

This chapter has shown that the individual man, as a member of the human race, has rights that must be respected beyond national frontiers. The Charter of the United Nations states that the protection of human rights is a fundamental international question. But for the time being, human rights are not yet international positive rights but only moral obligations. Perhaps one day the ideal will be realized and an authoritative international authority established where both individuals and States may defend their rights and claims.

CHAPTER FOUR

RACIAL IMAGES AND ATTITUDES IN BRITAIN—THE BACKGROUND

by

Sheila Patterson, M.A., DIP. ANTHROP.

Mrs Patterson is editor of the Newsletter of the
Institute of Race Relations, on whose staff she
has been since 1960. She is a social anthropologist who has carried out several studies of
minority and immigrant groups in South Africa
and Canada as well as studies in the absorption
of Polish and West Indian immigrants in
Britain.

Universalists, Élitists and Conformists

In 1953, a Dutch Reformed Church conference of Church leaders, meeting in Pretoria to discuss "Christian Principles in Multi-Racial South Africa", in its final statement categorized the viewpoints of participants under three different headings: those who sincerely believe in a righteous racial separation in the Church based on the scriptures; those who make no such confession but who nevertheless practise some form of separation because circumstances demand it; and those who are convinced that separation in the Church is wrong and stands condemned according to scripture.

This shows up a basic dichotomy within Christendom between the narrow ethnocentric viewpoint of the "élitists" or believers in a "chosen people" and the universalistic, supranational, supra-racial approach. It also illustrates the threefold division of attitudes and behaviour found in many societies, with the opinion-forming élitists and universalists at either pole and, in the middle, the mass of those whose views may be influenced by the beliefs of either or both groups, but who in behaviour conform to the prevailing social circumstances.

Unlike South Africa, there is in post-Christian Britain today no demographic, racial or socio-economic compulsion towards such a dichotomy or trichotomy. Yet the analysis has its value. In relation to foreigners, coloured immigrants and all outgroups, attitudes and behaviour on the whole fall into an intermediate "conformist" division of avoidance and mild xenophobia, with a philanthropic minority at one pole and a minority of ethnocentric "élitists" at the other.

In this chapter I shall attempt to indicate the major historical, socio-cultural, political and other elements which helped to produce the racial images and attitudes that still influence relations between coloured immigrants and local people in Britain today. For such images and attitudes often live on well beyond the ideas, emotions and situations that gave rise to them.

Three Strands in the European Heritage

The British and European conceptions of coloured peoples, and of non-Britons and non-Europeans in general, have been influenced not only by their philosophical, social and cultural heritage but also by their changing views of the nature of human society as a whole. These views have swung between the two opinion-forming poles over the centuries.

In Europe, as elsewhere, the popular awareness of biological differences or "social race" seems to have been a comparatively recent invention or rediscovery. It began to assume its present widespread importance only following the large-scale intercontinental migrations and confrontations of recent centuries. Before that, the stress fell far more heavily on social and cultural similarities or differences, although the idea of transmission down the generations probably implied some biological association.

The three major strands in Europe's cultural and philosophical heritage derive from Greece, Rome and Judaea. All three contained "universalistic" as well as "élitist" notions, although the latter were generally more stressed in relation to other peoples and cultures.

The ancient Greeks saw themselves and the rest of the world in cultural terms as Hellenes and Barbarians—people who did not speak Greek, or, more literally, "jabberers". There may have been a stronger "racial" ethnocentrism in Sparta, with its rigid divisions between citizens, Messenians, and Helots. But Alexander the Great, facing a series of conquests and expansions not unlike those faced by Spanish, Portuguese and later colonizers in Asia and Africa, interpreted his mission in cultural, not racial, terms.

In Rome we find a strong distinction between Roman and non-Roman in terms of citizenship and culture—but less concern, under the emperors, with ethnic origins. Some of the greatest of the emperors were born in remote provinces of non-Roman parents—one at least had a dark skin and came from Africa. In Rome, moreover, the frequency with which often unrelated children were adopted into patrician families suggests a definite belief in the supremacy of nurture over nature—environment over heredity.

Society in both Greece and Rome nevertheless possessed the institution of slavery and a hierarchy of social strata based to a considerable extent on descent—divisions that were most frequently justified in terms of a religious or metaphysical sanction. These institutions and divisions left a legacy of forms, ideas and mythological rationalizations which have not entirely ceased to influence our own world, and which were even more influential in the early days of European expansion overseas.

For instance, Aristotle, while recognizing economic stratification as between free citizens, regarded the division between free men and slaves as the basis dichotomy in the social structure. Moreover, he supported the view that this division had a natural basis in the types of human nature. St Augustine cited the curse which condemned sinful Ham to eternal bondage in the service of his worthy brothers, in order to show that slavery, though contrary to human nature, was justified by the sins which have warped man's nature. This myth of Ham was to prove very useful to various later élitist "establishments". It was used by the defenders of serfdom in the Middle Ages, by anti-abolitionist ministers in the Southern States, and by South African Calvinists seeking to justify first slavery and then *baas-kap* or white domination. Nor should the old religious dichotomy between white and black, good or evil, God and Satan be overlooked as a powerful influence which has reinforced "élitist" notions in many European languages.

In medieval England there was a religious sanction for the established order, expressed in the familiar verse:

> The rich man in his castle,
> The poor man at his gate,
> God made them high or lowly,
> And ordered their estate.

However, as the religious sanction weakened and the established order began to crack in the seventeenth and eighteenth centuries under the assaults of rationalism, some defenders of estate or class divisions began to express themselves in more specifically "racial" terms. In seventeenth-century France, Henri de Boulainvilliers evolved the theory that the French nobility was of Frankish or Teutonic origin, by contrast to the Gallo-Roman plebeians to whom the absolutist French kings looked for support in their attack on the liberties of the nobility. This mythical dichotomy is particularly worthy of note because it led to the Aryan theories of de Gobineau, who attributed the social decay which he discerned in nineteenth-century France to race mixture between qualitatively unequal races, and thereafter to the much more pernicious views of the germanised Englishman, Houston Stewart Chamberlain, the father of scientific racism.

In England there was a hint of "racial class" theorizing as early as the Cromwellian revolution, when it was argued by some that the Cavaliers represented the alien Norman tyranny which would be overthrown by the Saxon common people. Later Sir Walter Scott in *Ivanhoe* romanticized the class differences and struggles of feudal England in terms of "racial" conflict between Saxons and Normans—and Charles Kingsley in *Hereward the Wake* gave a Victorian view of the despicable "Milesians" or Celts.

Disraeli, too albeit in a specific political context, expressed the view that "everything is race", with the Jews—"a pure race of the Caucasian organization"—playing a particular and important role in European history. But perhaps a more significant comment of his was that about the formation of "two nations" within English society. This basically socio-economic conception, indicating the great gulf between rich and poor at that time, is today echoed in more explicitly racial terms by those who direly prophesy the formation of an under-class in Britain, distinguished from the rest of society by its colour.

To return to the third, Judaic strand in the European heritage, this is not the place to discuss how much of a racial element there was in the traditional, highly ethnocentric Jewish religion and culture. The mythology of the "chosen people" has, however, proved useful to later groups, particularly the Boers, and to certain fundamentalist religions in Britain and elsewhere —although this has not necessarily inclined them to adopt a favourable attitude towards the Jews of their own day. On the other hand, the earlier Judaeo-Christian view that all mankind was descended from a single pair for long buttressed universalist beliefs.

In medieval Europe anti-Semitism seems to have been explicable chiefly in religious and economic terms.

Apart from their specific and unpopular financial roles, the Jews were the only non-Christians within Christendom in a crusading era: they were also non-Christians who were accused of having killed Christ and of indulging in such practices as the ritual murder of Christian children. Moreover they were visually distinctive, culturally self-segregating, and increasingly isolated from the majority society residentially and by legal restrictions.

It is generally said of the "Latin" societies and cultures of France, Spain and Portugal that they have stressed cultural elements as against racial ones in their relations with minorities and subject peoples, in contrast to the Protestant societies of northern Europe. This is attributed to the universalistic legacy of Rome and the universalism of Roman Catholicism. There is considerable validity in this, yet the dichotomy between the "élite" and the "universalistic" conceptions emerges not only in religious but in racial terms even within such societies. It was after all in Spain that the Inquisition really took root after 1480. Furthermore its chief victims were not those who were heretics or impure of faith but those Jews and Moors who had been converted to Christianity (*conversos* and *moriscos*). This victimization was carried out under the statutes of *limpieza de sangre* (purity of blood). Only those of the right blood, it was maintained, could truly hold the right doctrines. "So", writes Hugh Trevor-Roper, "Spanish society was gradually changed. From an 'open', mixed society, in free contact with the outside world, it became a 'closed' society, turned in on itself, hating foreigners and 'novelty', clinging to its own values and

prejudices." No country could, it seems, avoid the great confusion that still bedevils the world—that between biological
race and "social" race, between genetic inheritance and
cultural transmission of a social heritage.

The European Heritage and the New World

The accumulated heritage of pre-colonial Europe contributed
to the cultural baggage that accompanied the adventurers, the
merchants, the conquerors and the missionaries who began to
stream out over the oceans in the fifteenth century. But that
heritage was also added to and changed in a number of ways by
the impact of new worlds, new peoples and new cultures. Moreover, notions and stereotypes began to evolve about these
peoples and cultures among the masses of Europeans who
stayed at home, and rarely if ever came into direct contact with
them.

These second-hand conceptions were, as has been said, influenced not only by the actual circumstances of contact, but also
by the changing climate of ideas in Europe In France and
England, both late-comers at the division of spoils in the new
worlds overseas, overseas expansion began not so very long
before the era of rationalism, with its eighteenth-century romanticized concomitant of the myth of the "noble savage".

The rationalist viewpoint was well put by the Scotsman
Adam Ferguson, who maintained that "polished nations" have
only an "air of superior ingenuity" in their success at the task of
civilization, and have no innate, but only a social, superiority to
the "savage in his forest". The image of the "noble savage",
with its revolutionary implications about the natural goodness
of man and the need to transform the existing faulty organization of society, was probably strongest in France although
Defoe drew such a picture for English readers in Robinson
Crusoe.

In Britain, the general approach tended to be more practical
and philanthropic. For instance, Samuel Johnson, a tradition-
alist who was also an opponent of slavery, was little impressed
by "cant in defence of savages", but he shocked the men of

Oxford by proposing a toast to "the next insurrection of the negroes in the West Indies".

As Negro slaves arrived in increasing numbers to serve in fashionable households, some absconding to the port settlements in which coloured seamen were already to be found, familiar-sounding complaints about their numbers, idleness, and refractoriness began to be heard. Nevertheless, little was said about supposed biological differences or inferiority until the last decades of the eighteenth-century.

Philanthropists and Pro-Slavers

At this stage, the growing hostility to the slave trade and slavery came to a head over the uncertain legal status of slaves in England. The anti-slavery and pro-slavery factions (the latter representing the West Indian slave-owners) began to muster their arguments. The first victory went to Granville Sharp on the anti-slavery side. This was the Somersett case of 1772, in which Lord Mansfield declared that slavery was not allowed or approved by the laws of England. Even at this time Granville Sharp thought it necessary, in preparing his case, to obtain scientific opinion as to whether the Negro, who as a slave was widely regarded as a form of property, was also a human being; this was included in his historic tract "On the Injustice and Dangerous Tendency of Tolerating Negro Slavery in England". At about the same time several serious attempts were made to justify the slave status of Negroes on the grounds that they were a different species of man, and wanting in the moral sense. In his *History of Jamaica* published in 1774, Mr Long wrote:

"We cannot pronounce them *unsusceptible of civilization, since even apes* have been taught to eat, drink, repose and dress *like men*. But of all the human species hitherto discovered, their *natural baseness of mind* seems to afford the least hope of their being (except by miraculous interposition of Divine Providence), so far refined as *to think* as well as act like men. . . ."

From this time onwards the more serious battle for total abolition and emancipation was joined and feeling in Britain ran high on both sides for much of the nineteenth century (long after abolition and emancipation in British territories). As Sir Richard Burton said of the African: " . . . before the Wilber-forcean age, he was simply a Negro. That trade which founded Liverpool, and which poured five million of sterling into the national pocket, marked him to the one class a Man and a Brother, to the other a Negro."

The philanthropists, abolitionists and missionaries won their battle with the abolition of the slave trade in 1807 and emancipation throughout the British colonies in 1833. Nevertheless, the spate of pro-slavery propaganda about the Negro as an inferior being, or a member of an inferior species, left its mark even on the philanthropists' attitudes. From the egalitarian viewpoint of the early eighteenth-century the image of the Negro had subtly shifted. He was now seen not as a noble savage but as a poor innocent benighted savage or heathen, to be patronized, protected and instructed in the true faith by the enlightened European.

This attitude, fostered up to our own times by some missionary societies, was expressed rather charmingly by the missionary Knibb in a speech to the Baptist Missionary Society in 1832:

"For nearly eight years I had trodden the sunburnt and slave-cursed island of Jamaica during which time your gratitude has been often called forth by the pleasing intelligence that God was blessing instrumentality employed. In almost every part of Jamaica Christian churches have been established, which may vie with any in the world for a devout attendance on the means of grace, and for the simple yet fervent zeal of their members.

"Hill and dale, street and hamlet, have resounded with the praise and prayer of the African who had been taught that Jesus died to save him, and the sweet simple strains of the many-coloured slave population have often sounded delightfully on our ears. Success has attended your missionaries in a manner which has appeared to promise the commencement of the millennium.

"But I need not say, that all is lost, that our harps are hung upon the willows, and that the voice of praise is no more heard in our streets. A combined Satanic effort has been made to root out all religion; the sanctuaries of God have been broken down with axes and hammers, and the infuriated yell, 'Rase it, rase it, even to the foundation thereof', has resounded through the island. Feeling, therefore, as I do, that the African and the Creole slave will never again enjoy the blessings of religious instruction, or hear of the benefits of that gospel which Christ has commanded to be preached among all nations, and which he has so eminently blessed in Jamaica, unless slavery be overthrown, I now stand forward as the unflinching and undaunted advocate of immediate emancipation."[1]

A nastier image, and one reminiscent of certain contemporary statements, was that given by Carlyle in his essay "The Nigger Question", published in 1849. While he would not wish to see them slaves again, they were the lowest of the human species and would decidedly "have to be servants to those that are born *wiser* than you, that are born lords of you; servants to the whites. . . ." The ex-slaves did not accept the duty of labour and the typical Negro was "poor Quashee . . . a merry-hearted, grinning, dancing, singing affectionate kind of creature, with a great deal of melody and amenability in his composition." This image has become blurred over a hundred years, but possibly it was in the minds of those West Indians who recently signed a petition asking for the "Black and White Minstrel Show" to be taken off television as injurious and offensive to coloured people.

So far from the ex-slaves lounging in comfortable idleness, however, the effect of the Mansfield decision in 1772 and of final emancipation in 1833 was to increase destitution amongst the Negroes in East London. They ceased to be an object of special concern or pity and, apart from some who continued to work as coachmen and footmen, joined the masses of the urban unskilled poor. Negrophile attitudes continued, especially among the aristocracy and upper middle classes, but it was generally directed at distant targets. As C. M. Macinnes wrote in *England and Slavery* (Arrowsmith 1934):

"The majority of English men could afford to be zealous in

[1] *Sources of West Indian History*, by F. R. Augier and S. C. Gordon, Longmans 1962, pp. 156–7.

the negro's interests, since so few of them were affected in their pockets by a campaign which threatened ruin to the plantations. It was much easier to be sympathetic and broadminded about negroes in Jamaica . . . than to protest against the sufferings of English women and children who were daily sacrificed in the mills on the altar of the new industrialism."

Kenneth Little (*Negroes in Britain*, Kegan Paul 1948, p. 207) also stresses the ambivalent attitudes of philanthropists, but adds a comment on the generally tolerant attitudes of the mass of British workers. "Despite this the Negro seems to have raised extraordinarily little exasperation even among those who had least reason to pity him."

To help explain this relative tolerance we must refer briefly to a contemporary set of beliefs and a political movement that had little connection with other nations or races but was concerned with changing the nature of British society itself. This was the British social democratic movement which, apart from earlier flickers of internationalism and revolutionary ardour, evolved a specifically insular flavour. It was non-doctrinaire, empirical, reformist and gradualist. Individual liberty, dignity, independence and self-help were among its chief values, and it had an enduring strain of religiosity that distinguished it from most Continental working-class movements. Rooted in British conditions, the British working class movement had a general sympathy with workers in other countries which might even be extended to those who came here. The principle of universal brotherhood could nevertheless be strained. Seventy years ago Ben Tillett told newly-arrived Jewish immigrant workers: "Yes, you are our brothers and we will do our duty by you. But we wish you had not come to this country." This classic statement neatly illustrates the ambivalence of attitudes that still characterizes much of organized British labour.

"Social Darwinism" and "White Superiority"
Anthropological theories played an increasing part in the emancipation debate and the general formation of images and attitudes. The philanthropists had espoused the monogenist

theory, which maintained that all mankind was descended from a single origin. The pro-slavery propagandists of Britain and America drew on the theory of the polygenists, who had as a consequence of the discoveries of new peoples and new cultures revived an old belief that the different races were of separate origins. In 1863 the debate led to the secession from the Ethnological Society of a group of supporters of the polygenistic interpretation. Its leader gave an address on "The Negro's Place in Nature", in which he maintained that the Negro was a different species from the European, inferior intellectually, with many more analogies to the ape than the latter, and that European civilization was not suited to the Negro's requirements or character. This thesis was not well received in Britain, but it may have lingered on in blurred and unfocused form.

In any case, the monogenist-polygenist dispute was destined for the scientific scrap-heap. In 1859 Charles Darwin's work *The Origin of Species by Means of Natural Selection; or, The Preservation of Favoured Races in the Struggle for Life* shot down both theories and established a new monogenist theory, according to which man was the ultimate product of a long and incalculable process of steady differentation. Darwin later dealt with selection in the human species, but made no attempt to classify races, finding the races of man puzzling and differing in every physical character in regard to which individuals are known to vary.

Darwin's doctrine of natural selection as the driving force behind development supplied, as Michael Banton writes, the "missing foundation stone for Herbert Spencer's theory of evolution". It also suited the social temper of the age, in which a new scramble for Empire was looming. The result was "social Darwinism", whose propagandists, less scientific and less cautious than Darwin himself, attempted to translate Darwin's doctrines into a law of social development. Stronger nations tended to prevail over others and stronger nations tended to be better. This led to an association of the ideas of nation and race, an affirmation of the innate superiority of the Aryan, Nordic and Teutonic races, and the assumption of a socio-cultural hierarchy of races. Ralph Linton in *The Study of Man* suggests that the theory of evolution replaced previous rationalizations justifying the domination of the white races. Since the latter had survived and been more successful than the other races, they must be superior to them, not only in organization and efficiency, but in every other field, including the mental and moral.

Imperialism and Jingoism

This trend of thinking was to lead, via the anthropo-sociologists of Germany and France (Ammon and Lapauge out of de Gobineau via Wagner), to Teutonic chauvinism and Pan-Germanism, and to help fortify the Anglo-Saxon imperialism and jingoism of the end of the nineteenth-century.

Michael Banton quotes the historian, John Adam Cramb, as arguing, during a series of lectures given at the time of the South African War, that imperialism is "patriotism transfigured by a light from the aspirations of universal humanity . . . in a race dowered with the genius for empire, Imperialism is the supreme, the crowning form, which in this process of evolution it attains." He went on to speak portentously of the looming "war of races . . . which will touch to purposes yet higher and more mystic the wars of empires"—a simple sentiment of which variants are still to be heard from those analysts of contemporary events who, whether racist or liberal in motivation, abjure the multi-factorial approach.

In Britain, however, despite the writings of Karl Pearson (the biological theory of the State, the genetic poverty of the Negro stock, and the colonization of waste lands with "our own kith and kin", even at the expense of "an inferior race of inhabitants") and those of Madison Grant (*The Passing of the Great Race*), the jingoistic spirit and its rationalizations lasted only a few decades.

Again, some diluted traces lingered, though rather as a form of folklore than as a major set of beliefs. Even in the case of the minority of Britons and others directly concerned with the administration of Empire, the expansionist self-righteous jingoism of the later nineteenth-century gradually changed among many into an unaggressive, responsible paternalism. By the 1930's a critical student of colonialism, Leonard Barnes, could admit that the modern official, with all his limitations, was remarkably free from jingo sentiment, and viewed with wholesome scepticism the old "clap-trap" about Empires designed to spread European enlightenment in the dark places of the earth. "He sees himself, not as an Empire builder, but as a builder and decorator of native societies."

Aftermath of Empire

This transformation of attitudes and approach accompanied an overall shift in the idea of Empire, from the harsher conceptions of Rhodes and Milner, to the more genial, if short-lived, afterglow of the "old" Commonwealth club as seen by Smuts, Churchill, Mackenzie King and Menzies. Then came the period of decolonization and disillusionment, and the return of the colonial exiles; of "post-colonial" blues, diminished national status and the as yet vain search for a new role. To quote Elspeth Huxley, commenting on the opposition to the Commonwealth Immigrants Act of 1962:

"Most people on the idealistic wing of our society opposed this Act on grounds of principle. Our long tradition of free entry by any citizens of the Commonwealth must not (they said) be broken; we are the heart and centre of the Commonwealth and must not deny to anyone its open shores. Here crops up, again, the image of the mother who has sent forth her sons and mustn't slam the door in the face of any who want to come home.

"This is, alas, at bottom an imperialist, paternalistic notion, and it's ironical that the most anti-imperialist of our thinkers should be the ones to voice it most emphatically. Broken and tarnished lies the mother-image; Asians and Africans never were her sons, anyway; her dugs are dry.

"What is the Commonwealth, held up to the raw light of day? An idea in minds that, like all human minds, recoil from uncongenial reality, such as the loss of power and glory, and want to go on believing that as things were, so they remain.

c

A sort of mummy-case in which we have embalmed an empire that's dead but that we can't bring ourselves finally to bury, because we want to go on feeling that something's still there."[1]

All the beliefs and images outlined here have left a set of blurred and muddled traces on public opinion and attitudes in Britain. Yet, as Kenneth Little points out, they carried conviction mainly among intellectuals and litterateurs, and probably had little effect on the common man: "The general public has never had much patience with abstract notions of race and racial superiority, and . . . in recent times it is more likely that the general belief in 'Civilisation' and the whole philosophy of 'progress' . . . was far more conclusive in justifying psychologically, and apparently concretely, what the racialists claimed in less understandable language."

This distinction between the attitudes of the "élite", whether liberal or ethnocentric, and those of the general public can still be made today. The latter, apart from their general indifference to and ignorance about Commonwealth matters, tend to take a more pragmatic view, whether it is of "wogs" met casually in Asian and African ports during service in the armed forces, or of coloured immigrants competing for jobs and houses in Britain. Their attitudes may, however, be conditioned by notions of strangeness and inferiority acquired from outmoded textbooks and ill-informed middle-class teachers.

Nevertheless, these attitudes are generally not rigidly stereotyped but susceptible to modification by first-hand experience. It is mainly among the middle classes and the aspirants to this status that the out-moded preconceptions derived from the imperialist, missionary and pseudo-anthropological thinking of the nineteenth century still linger. Among liberal intellectuals, this sometimes emerges in an unconscious hangover of philanthropic patronage and an apparent concentration on the problems and difficulties of "coloured" immigrants.

[1] *Back Street New Worlds—A Look at Immigrants in Britain*, Chatto and Windus 1964, pp. 152–3.

These attitudes, like those of some nineteenth-century philan-thropists, invite charges of hypocrisy from the local white people who have faced the same difficulties and problems for years. Such people rarely feel a need to make amends for imperialistic wrongs, although they may have a fellow-feeling for those who suffered them. It was not, after all, their Empire, they will say. They did not win it or oppress its peoples and yet it is they who are expected to welcome the products of exploitation, the immigrant work-seekers from the West Indies and Asia, as workers and residents in the overcrowded twilight areas of Britain's large cities.

Factors for Change

Santayana wrote: "The Englishman is no missionary, no conqueror. He prefers the country to the town and home to foreign parts. He is rather glad and relieved if only natives will remain natives and strangers strangers, and at a comfortable distance from himself."

It is often, and truly, said that mild xenophobia is a cultural norm among the British, or rather the English. The attitude is one of avoidance rather than aggression and it applies not only to outsiders but to out-groups within the society, between North and South, between one village and another, even between neighbouring streets. It goes back over many centuries of village life, historical and cultural continuity and insular isolation. For many hundreds of years the majority of Britons have met non-Britons only in times of war, as enemies or rather unwelcome allies, in the colonial situation or as unwelcome competitors for work imported by unscrupulous employers to threaten jobs and keep living standards down.

The recent coloured immigrants fall into the last two cate-gories, as colonials in the wrong place and as competitors for jobs. Furthermore, their visible strangeness, which made them seem to be the supreme and ultimate strangers, has been accen-tuated by a set of historical preconceptions associating colour with alien culture and low socio-economic status.

In recent years some of the superficial strangeness has worn off; coloured faces, turbans and saris have become an accepted part of the urban landscape if not yet of the community. The customary processes of accommodation are at work in factories, neighbourhoods, schools and elsewhere. Situations and attitudes are still flexible, despite periodic peaks of ethnocentric resentment and apprehension on both sides, as in 1958 and 1965.

At present there seems to be a race against time, to prevent attitudes from hardening into a rigid association of colour with low status before the coloured second-generation can succeed in spreading out into the skilled and clerical jobs, the better streets and the suburban estates. Because of the lost years of *laissez-faire*, and the fact that this particular immigration has been identified with the world-wide issues of race and colour, legislation and other official measures have become essential to induce a conformity of non-discrimination.

Yet the long-term trends of development in British society permit of a reasonably positive prognosis. There is a slow movement towards a more egalitarian, open-class pattern, and an increasing tolerance of religious and ethnic minorities and of other cultures. The greatest single factor for change, the schools and universities, are acquiring a less narrow and ethnocentric approach. Young people are increasingly outward-looking and in touch with their contemporaries in Europe and the Third World of independent "coloured" nations. Whether the motivation is religious, political or scientific, the overall trend seems to be away from the "élitist" and towards the "universalistic" view of the world and Britain's place in it. The notion of "white superiority" is dead or dying—although the counter-notion of "black power" may yet have some years to run.

CHAPTER FIVE

THE PSYCHOLOGY OF PREJUDICE

by

David Stafford-Clark, M.D., F.R.C.P., D.P.M.

Dr Stafford-Clark is Consultant Physician, Department of Psychological Medicine, Guy's Hospital; Consultant Physician, Maudsley and Bethlem Royal Hospital; Director of the York Clinic, Guy's Hospital, London.

This chapter is based upon an original lecture first given as the Robert Waley Cohen Memorial Lecture in 1960, delivered under the auspices of the Council of Christians and Jews, at the University of London, and subsequently published by them in pamphlet form.

Definition

Wherever and however it is encountered, racial intolerance remains the same terrible thing, no matter what its source or whomsoever its victims. Our first task must be to examine the basis of prejudice and persecution in the relationship between man and man, and to trace this through biological and psychological evidence to its final and challenging implications, with their inevitably tragic outcome unless the facts are faced, the implications acknowledged, and previous assumptions and attitudes fundamentally altered.

The biological homogeneity of the human race is undisputed. In the Bible (Acts xvii. 26), we are told that God created all nations of one kind of man; and geneticists, anthropologists and biologists, would agree that man is of one species; but they would also agree that there are a number of races of that species. We must presently consider the precise implications of that statement: but what is immediately tragically and painfully apparent is that this division into racial groups has from time immemorial been the focus of so much inherent antipathy, cruelty, rancour, arrogance, hatred, spite, and all that sheer uncharitableness which so often mars the relationship of human beings with each other.

Prejudice has been defined in *Webster's Dictionary* as "An unreasonable, or unjustifiably adverse opinion without just grounds or sufficient knowledge." Persecution is "To pursue so as to injure, grieve or afflict." Now those simple words conjure up a very lively image in our minds of what those two states mean; of what it is to be the victim of prejudice, and of what it is to be persecuted. In the relations of human beings to each other there can of course be no final justification for either activity.

It is never, and it can never be, justifiable to pursue so as to injure, grieve or afflict another human being; still less, by definition alone, can it ever be justifiable to hold "an unreasonably adverse opinion of anybody, without just grounds or sufficient knowledge"; and yet this is the way we find ourselves behaving. We must ask ourselves whence comes the ominous way that people feel about this? Whence the hostility? Whence the misgiving? Let us return for a moment to the Bible, and there turn, as traditionally we are invited, to the ant for an illustration.

Automatic Discrimination

Ants are creatures which probably have not more than 15 per cent. of their total behaviour in any way under their conscious control. By far the most of it seems to be innate, instinctive, automatic, and unreasoning, although very highly complicated. It is therefore interesting to note that ants can recognize members of their own colony, apparently by scent, and that they can and do avoid members of other colonies, particularly on foraging expeditions; that ants frequently make a particular kind of food for their colony by using various scraps of vegetable matter on which a particular mould will grow, taking from it a crop as men will take their corn. And if you then give an ant from one colony some of the crop from another colony, he will tend to refuse it.

Ants have in fact social prejudices, and prejudices about food. The work of Professor Tinbergen, formerly of Leyden University, now at Oxford, has shown that animals' behaviour is, to a remarkable degree, governed by what he calls "releasers". These are specific stimuli which release in the animal already innate patterns of activity. One of the reasons why mixture between different species seems to occur comparatively rarely in nature, is that releasers from one species are not represented by any activity of another.

The patterns of releaser activity in animals are indeed fascinating and complicated. An example is the mating pattern of the stickleback. A stickleback may begin its mating pattern with another little fish of approximately the same kind, but because the other little fish has an instinctive way of reacting to this, which differs from that of the stickleback itself, nothing comes of it. Neither decision, choice, nor even conscious

reasoning are called for here. Nevertheless, there is in fact no outcome: segregation has prevailed. But, on the other hand, take a
stickleback, put him in a glass test tube, place him in a part of
the tank which he normally inhabits, introduce another stickleback similarly enclosed in a test tube beside him, and the other
stickleback will immediately show all the evidence of an urgent
desire to flee. He will start waving his fins vigorously, while the
stickleback who is on his own ground will put his nose down and
tail up, adopting the attacking position as Tinbergen has
described it.

Reverse the geographical situation by transposing these two
in their respective test tubes to the other end of the tank where
the former intruder is now at home, and the former defender
of his territory is now on foreign soil, and although they can
have no other communication with each other, the change in
their environment releases precisely the opposite reactions in
each of them. The formerly pugnacious stickleback will now
try to flee, the former would-be fugitive will now become
aggressive. Their environment, in fact, acts as a releaser, to
which they in turn react automatically.

Tinbergen has drawn attention to the characteristic behaviour
of members of a group of social animals, towards one of their
number temporarily isolated, threatened or made "different"
in some disturbing way.

During the process of attaching coloured leg rings to individual herring gulls, so that he could identify them on future
occasions in the course of observing the whole colony, he was
struck by the behaviour of the rest of the colony towards the
temporarily netted gull, furiously struggling in a hitherto
unrecognized and perhaps seemingly dangerous predicament.
He has written:

"The gulls seemed to show a double response. On the one
hand they are alarmed by the disturbance. I think I have
heard the alarm call on a number of such occasions. On the
other hand their reaction to the captured gull seems defin-
itely hostile. It is known in other instances too that social

animals may attack individuals that behave in a different or abnormal manner.

"One is tempted to compare this with human behaviour. In human society, 'primitive' as well as 'civilised', a similar instinctive reaction is very strongly developed. It is perhaps possible to distinguish three steps or gradations of rising intensity in the social defence attitude of a crowd. The first is laughing at an individual who behaves in a slightly abnormal way. This reaction serves the function of forcing the individual back into the normal, that is to say, into conventional behaviour. The next and higher intensity reaction is withdrawal; the individual has made himself 'impossible' and his companions ignore him. This, viewed from the aspect of biological significance, is a still stronger stimulus to the abnormal person to behave normally. The highest intensity reaction is one of definite hostility, resulting in making the individual an outcast, and in primitive societies even in killing him. In my opinion, it is of great importance for human sociology to recognize the instinctive basis of such reactions and to study them comparatively in other social species."

Some alternative to this innate instinctive pattern of behaviour, whereby we first deride, then reject, and finally perhaps even attack the individual whose behaviour we do not or cannot accept, even the individual who differs from us in some striking or characteristic way, is of course essential if we are to raise ourselves above the level of animals in the way in which ultimately we treat each other.

Somerset Maugham's observation of the instinctive link between disability, difference and derogation, found telling expression on his story of the man with the club foot who always knew when he was winning an argument because his opponent would begin to call him a "club-footed bastard". Here again the point is that any recognition of difference is immediate and instinctive raw material for defamation; and whether the discrimination is based upon deformity or racial derivation, it is equally shameful.

We have seen that in animals the capacity for discrimination is apparently innate and instinctive, and the reaction automatic and all too often hostile. How much can this teach us about the roots of prejudice in human beings? Unlike most animals we are capable of some degree of insight into our own behaviour, into our motives and rationalizations, as well as our actions. Given our marvellously elaborate brains, our capacity for introspection and abstraction, our well-stocked minds, our vast and flexible power of symbolic thought, what have we turned up on this subject? For we have certainly thought about it often, even if not ever enough.

William Temple, the late Archbishop of Canterbury, wrote:

"When we open our eyes as babies we see the world stretching out around us. We are in the middle of it . . . I am the centre of the world I see and where the horizon is depends on where I stand. Now just the same thing at first is true of our mental and spiritual vision so each of us takes his place in the centre of his own world. But I am not the centre of the world or the standard of reference as between good and bad; I am not and God is. In other words, from the beginning I put myself in God's place. This is my original sin. I was doing it before I could speak, and everyone else has been doing it from early infancy."

These are certainly some of the factors contributing to the ultimate strength and complexity of human racial prejudice. Writing of them in his brilliant thesis "The Nature of Prejudice", Gordon Allport said,

"There is no master key. Rather what we have at our disposal is a ring of keys, each of which opens one gate of understanding".

But when we examine this ring of keys we find that the master key which might be constructed from them is still missing. There is a reason for this. I believe that it is to be found in certain assumptions made about human beings which I think it is our duty to examine critically for a moment.

Capacity to Love and Proclivity to Hate

I was first made aware of these assumptions some time ago when lecturing to parent/teacher groups. The lectures dealt among other things with such topics as juvenile delinquency, the natural rebelliousness of adolescence, and indeed the total impact of the conflict between self-love, and love of parents and others, in childhood. Often after such a lecture, starry-eyed and charming ladies came up to me and said, "But, doctor, isn't it sad; because all these little ones were born perfect and we must have corrupted them."

This is a monumental fallacy. The assumption is that malice and resentment are not inherent in us; that no one is born prejudiced; that no child comes into the world hating or ready to hate a child of another race. Now this of course is partly true, but it isn't the whole truth. Man is born certainly without established malice or resentment, he is born moreover with a need to love and to be loved. But together with the capacity to love there is the proclivity to hate; and we need to see what are the circumstances in which this proclivity is aroused.

Alas, they are simple enough. When we are crossed, frustrated, disappointed, or thwarted in any way, then we are ready to hate; and to hunt; and never more explosively than in infancy. Professor Lewis once said that if a tiny baby was as strong, powerful and decisive as a grown-up man, he would be the most dangerous creature on the face of the earth. He wants what he wants, when he wants it, immediately and unconditionally, and he will do everything in his power to get it. And his rage is just as impressive as his delight. So perhaps we must recast that statement about the infant's blessed freedom from prejudice and shape it nearer, if not to our heart's desire, at least to the truth. It would then have to read: "*No one is born prejudiced against others; but everyone is born prejudiced in favour of himself.* . . ."

So man is not born free of the capacity for prejudice.

Aggressive self-assertiveness is present from birth onwards. It is fundamental, we cannot escape it, it is part of us just as the releasers and the patterns of recognition are part of the ants and the gulls. Race prejudice is learned, religious bigotry is learned; but they can be learned only because they have an apt and inherent pupil in the prideful and instinctively self-willed aggressive aspect of each one of us.

Here we begin to get a clue. Psychologically and sociologically we can say that perhaps the soundest and most generally applicable theory to explain tension and hostility between different groups of human beings, is what is called the frustration-aggression theory. When we cannot achieve what we want, when we are disappointed, when our hopes outrun our attainments, when somebody else gets the job, or the girl, or the money, we would like to be able to tell ourselves that it wasn't our fault; that they had an unfair advantage; that if we had started with whatever particular gifts or luck they had, or if they hadn't been around, we would have done better. And indeed psychologically the same kind of mood and the same kind of frustration makes the thwarted child stamp the floor, the sacked workman kick his dog, the discouraged salesman blame his wife, the Gentile defame the Jew, the Jew despise the Gentile, the white man deride the Negro and now, the African put his gun into the back of the white man and demand his pass.

Cruelty and bestiality in the way human beings treat each other are not always confined to those who have the upper hand, for we are all in this; and we are all to blame. For the Christian there is an echo of an old lesson here; for he is bound to recognize that man is of infinite value, but that in his human condition he is not, and never will be, perfect; that he comes into the world ready to be hateful and aggressive as well as to be loving and appreciative and kind. Little children are indeed, born free from racial prejudice, but not from aggression.

Now in the social setting in which we live there are always people whom we can make the natural targets of these aggressive feelings. They are those of whom we can say "They are not of our kind". And to some extent it is a temptation not only to make such people scapegoats but to thank God that we are not as they are. There could be no greater insult to our concept of a God of all mankind than this kind of sanctimonious, hypocritical, complacent gratitude. But not even our concept of God can escape question or indictment in the context of this examination of the human predicament. As Hemingway put it,

"You did not know what it was about. You never had time to learn. They threw you in and told you the rules and the first time they caught you off base they killed you".

There is something in this. As human beings we start with a much bigger handicap than many of us realize. To the extent that sociological studies suggest to us that we are wholly social creatures, essentially conditioned by environment, I think they mislead us.

We have tended in the past to lay the blame for racial prejudice upon everything except the essential nature of the human personality; and have sought its solution eveywhere except in a radical change of that essential nature. The sociological error is in this respect a fundamental error, starting from the false assumption that man, reduced to his essential self, is ultimately a social unit and can therefore be wholly explained and only explained by social observations.

The Christian correction of this would be that the various keys to prejudice all hang from one ring, and that this ring is the innate, inevitable, yet tragic self-centredness of the human personality. So much of what emerges as evil in man is indeed the product of his inherent nature, in conflict with his inescapable environment, that we cannot afford to neglect a single indication of the true nature of prejudice and persecution.

Prejudice and Insanity

There is, for example, a striking resemblance between the embraced prejudice and the insane delusion; between persecution and psychotic behaviour; between the method of apartheid and the madness of paranoia.

Certainly prejudice and certain kinds of psychosis have this in common, that they are rigid against rational assault, yet flow round and by-pass the facts; and that they ignore arguments and refutations, however sound and convincing, as though they did not exist. Ask anybody who is convinced that racial segregation is the right answer to a social problem, for their grounds; begin to question them intelligently and politely, and almost always they will become angry with you, because you are attacking something which is fundamentally dear to them, which is important to them, which is a part of themselves.

Prejudice cannot be defended rationally; but then of course it never is; it is defended emotionally. The patterns shift and change, vary and fluctuate, but at the centre is always *self*. Men of all races alike are adept at this kind of rationalization. Indeed we have no need to pretend that Jews, Gentiles, Asians, Africans and Europeans cannot in their own way be just as critical, just as contemptuous of one another just as arrogant in their attitudes.

Bitterness and hostility are sustained by rationalizations combining fantastic ignorance with delusional conviction. Richard Hughes' Scottish Engineer, with his confident assertions about the anatomical peculiarities of the Chinese is a vivid example— with a typical conclusion.

"It's a scientific fact that a Chinaman has fewer nerves in his body than a white man. They can't feel pain. They're nearer to beasts than men, they are."

It is often said that foxes enjoy being hunted or that fishes can't feel the hook. Personally I cannot endorse either of these statements. We simply don't know, but I have no reason to suppose that a fish cannot feel the hook, I have no reason to suppose that a fox enjoys being hunted, but I do know the same number of nerves traverse the body of a Chinaman as of a Jew, as of an Arab, as of a Negro, as of a Caucasian (if you care for the term).

Sense of Superiority

Prejudice is bolstered by false information because of the prejudiced man's necessity to hang on to the idea that there is a difference in his favour between him and the rest of the world. Racial pride is ultimately simply a manifestation of the individual's innate sense of personal superiority; something he either believes or wishes to believe; something that rejects all that lies outside the hard core of his own self-centred will and desire. And this, tragically, is man's constant need, constantly supplied. Throughout history the Jew has had his Gentile, the Greek his Barbarian, the Crusaders their Infidels, the English had their Irish, the Irish their English, the Nazis their non-Aryans, the white man his Negro.

Prejudice is mercilessly necessary and as morally corrosive to the prejudiced man, as alcohol is to the alcoholic. Moreover prejudice inevitably becomes to the prejudiced what alcohol becomes to the alcoholic; not a problem but a solution. In this sense prejudice is a drug of addiction; and like every other object of addiction, like cigarettes, drink or drugs, it becomes indispensable to the addicted subject; part of the very essence of existence, the thing that makes him feel worth while. Take it away and he is unbearably distressed and diminished. Only by the implications of prejudice is the prejudiced man's own image of himself sustained. Only in the mirror of the aspersions which he casts on others can he see the distorted reflection of what he calls himself. Yet this is his tragedy no less than the tragedy of others.

Writing in the *Observer* on Sunday 10 May 1960, Miss Hannah Stanton had this to say:

"Because I was going to South Africa I read Father Huddleston's book, *Naught for your Comfort*, and while much admiring both the man and the message, felt that the picture it gave of the situation in South Africa was exaggerated, and that it was necessary for people like me to go to South Africa with an open mind.

"A fellow passenger on the boat got into conversation with me and took very much the 'Huddleston line', as I would probably have described it at that time. I remember thinking and saying to her, 'Yes, but there must be another side to it'.

"I managed to preserve this kind of 'detachment'—I put the word into inverted commas because I am not so sure now that the state of mind deserves the moral and intellectual compliments which the term detachment implies—for several weeks. Soon after I got there I spoke in the street to an African whom I know, and shook him by the hand.

" 'You can't do that here,' a passing white woman exclaimed. I went on talking. The white woman's tone became hysterical. 'You can't do that here,' she repeated. 'Do you hear me? You must be from overseas. You can't do that here.' But she moved on and I finished my conversation.

"It was embarrassing and difficult to reconcile it with an ordinary sense of people's prejudices, however deep. It was difficult and embarrassing, also, to meet the eyes of Africans standing in fantastically long queues, waiting to get on to buses, or waiting while the whites were served in banks and shops, while I was so obviously a member of a class as privileged as they were humiliated."

Political Expediency

To justify this kind of attitude, to make racial prejudice the basis of a philosophy, or to pervert it into a foundation for a religious belief, is to commit yet one more atrocious, terrible, tragic crime against all the standards that men between them have ever managed to erect. And yet, of course, politically it is sometimes expedient. If political expediency has achieved nothing else, it will surely have made us aware that standards which transcend such expediency are necessary, if we are to survive. Political expediency finds racial prejudice a very handy weapon for producing policies which not only politicians but indeed many of their followers are only too willing to believe are helpful. For when there is trouble it is expedient that there should be a scapegoat; and once again the innate self-centredness, the hard core within each one of us is enabled to say "Well, it's not my fault and I don't see why I should suffer. It's too bad for *them*, but then *we* were here first (or) this is *our* country (or) *we've* always been to these schools; *we* don't want *them* coming here."

There are other factors which whip this up; those amoral factors in a society which haplessly affect its entire moral balance. Given a lot of people who are readily distinguishable because of their colour, or their background, or their racial or cultural characteristics, easily and openly identifiable, who have already drifted into a society which they have believed to be golden, but which in fact finds it hard to provide them with work and homes, and you are saddled not simply with their own misery; but with the hatred, cruelty and arrogant projection of hostility upon them which this insensitively competitive social situation produces.

It was a salutary but terrible lesson that we in this country, who knew so much better than the people of Little Rock or the people of Cape Town how to deal with our brothers, began to learn when we found ourselves with broken windows and broken hearts in Notting Hill Gate. I dare to predict without hesitation but not without misgiving that if we were now to hit a slump, to have to endure a lot of unemployment, if the housing situation suddenly became crucially bad, the first people to be blamed and brutally treated would be our coloured immigrants, who came here because they believed that here they would be well treated; that here they would be able to earn a respectable living in a respectable way.

Of course they behave badly sometimes; in reaction to the treatment they receive or out of ignorance of the customs of their new society. Among their instinctive human reactions to cruelty and prejudice are included not only undue submissiveness with loss of self-respect; but, alternatively, deceitful indifference as a cloak for reciprocal arrogance and aggression.

These evils are part of the inevitable price to be paid for

persecution; of which enforced segregation is but a special example. As Kyle Haselden has written:

"Racial segregation is a temporal behaviour which assumes it has cancelled the eternal fact of the oneness of man. It separates on the social, or economic, or civil level that which cannot be separated in the deeper reaches of the human soul. And the result for white man and Negro is an illness, the illness of those who are estranged from those to whom they belong. For however fine we may draw out the nerve which connects man to man, it does not break. If it did, all the agonies, the aches and sorrows of human separation would break with it; but it does not break; it holds forever, thin and taut; and along this nerve throb the anxieties, the fears, the pangs of human estrangement.

"From the anxieties of this separation the white man has in the past tried to escape, not by restoring and completing the broken union, but by seeking to make the severance complete."

This is the moral philosophy of Apartheid—and it is not confined to any one society. The agonies of the victim of segregation are the agonies of suffocation, because he is cut off from the source and expression of the fullness of life, by being segregated from that to which he belongs. To the extent that he cannot wholly and finally identify himself with all his fellow human beings, he is made to feel unwanted and unloved, and that is the most destructive thing that can be inflicted upon a human being.

But the effect upon the segregator is ultimately even worse. In the expression of vicious and passionate racial prejudice, the segregator ultimately surrenders to the beast within himself. Newspaper pictures of the jeering, spitting, stone-throwing crowds which have resisted the de-segregation of public schools in the southern States of America are dreadful evidence of this fact, and of the atmosphere of unconscious stereotyping. The white man becomes, in regard to the Negro, an amoral character.

By making something human alien to himself, he inevitably diminishes his own humanity, and the fact that he does not know this, is indeed the measure of its destructive effects upon his own soul. The first tragedy of many passively but unreflectingly prejudiced people in their relationship to the victims of their prejudice, is not that they are passionately alive towards the victim in hatred or contempt, but they are dead towards him in understanding, identity of feeling and simple compassion. This death is within the privileged rather than in the excluded. Unwilling to let the victim be, he denies, degrades and finally destroys himself.

So, undeniably, there must be an alternative. But what is it? Before we suppose it to be simple liberalism, we must return for the last time in this chapter to an honest examination of ourselves, of the dark places in our own hearts. By all means let us rise above our primitive animal releasers; let us abandon our ant-like behaviour, our herring gull attitude; but then how far are we prepared to go? And what will this demand of us?

Intermarriage

Here I think we come to the heart of the matter; that ultimately fundamental blend of human and animal feeling, capable of the greatest degree of intensity: the sexual instinct. For this may prove the crucial touchstone to our attitude.

By all means, we may say, let's be liberal, let's have no more segregation, let's not mind whether the hand that we shake is a different colour to our own. Let's ask the Gentiles to our celebrations, the Negroes to our parties; let's have a society in which we mingle freely. And then one of our opponents, one of these bigoted people, will confront us with the old, old question: "All right, how'd you feel if your daughter was going to marry a Negro?" Or to a Negro, "How'd you feel if your daughter was going to marry one of those white men who has just broken one of your windows?" Until we can say that we should approach this in exactly the same frame of mind as we should the prospective marriage of our daughter to any other human being, then we are not facing this problem.

It is my own sincere and personal belief that the future of the human race is constantly to intermingle; and in this at least I am consistent. Some of the finest people I have ever known were the product of mixed racial ancestry. I do not proclaim, because I do not know, that hybridization is indispensable to the greatest vitality of the human species, but I can say without hesitation that biologically it does no harm. If we shrink from it, our misgivings are not based upon facts, but upon feelings.

We have seen something of the psychological origin of these feelings and so we need not be surprised at any inconsistencies in their expression. In the southern States of America, for example, it has long been a traditional convention of white male virility to have had sexual intercourse with a coloured girl some time or another before marriage; of course, without public acknowledgement, still less with any investment of personal responsibility. But just let this sexual miscegenation occur the other way round, and the outrage, the horror, leads immediately to appalling violence. Yet basically, both are biologically identical procedures.

Intermarriage between all human races is biologically, and I dare to suggest spiritually, not only defensible but right. Hybridization at a biological level enriches natural diversity and tends to produce a more versatile genetic structure. It cannot of itself be a bad thing.

But the life which is led at the moment by the Anglo-Indians, by the high-yellows, by the Cape-coloureds, is a standing reproach not to them, but to those who despise, reject, persecute and oppress them; in the name of their own delusional superiority, to which they cling with the fierce, devoted, savage intensity of the prejudiced persecutors. Yet there is no evil, in my view, greater than the organized, persistent and strongly maintained prejudice, that one human being can have against another. And miscegenation would be a very small price to pay for the end of that, if indeed it is regarded as a price at all.

The Central Problem

And so finally, let us attempt to grapple with the implications of this problem as it explosively emerges. If biologically miscegenation is an acceptable and possible solution why is it the one thing that everybody strives against?

I think one of the reasons is that we cannot bear to admit that others, different from ourselves as we see them to be, are as good as we are. We set too high a value on ourselves and too low a value on human beings as a whole: this is the universal problem. Study the psychological development of the infant. The most important, the most fundamental need that the infant has after being born is to be able to differentiate himself from the rest of the world; between that aspect of his experience which is constantly part of him and, although ever-changing, goes with him wherever he goes, and that part which he comes to recognize as ineffably separate and distinct from him. His most fundamental lesson is in fact to recognize his own separateness, his identity, which in fact he will later learn to call "me"; my body, my feelings, my thoughts, as something distinct from the whole of the rest of the world; which, infinitely varied, wonderful, packed with no matter what challenges, delights or possibilities, is not "me".

This "me/not me" differentiation is made instinctively, inevitably, and indeed of necessity, and where it isn't made, it may well be that normal development is impossible. Until we know that we exist in our own right we can't make our way in the world at all. Yet the mystics have always said, and the Eastern philosophers are always saying, that this really is the fundamental, the basic error of us all: that in truth man is one with the Universe and that until he recognizes and achieves that sense of oneness and wholeness and reabsorption, he is never fully aware of what he is or what life is.

So we are kept stumbling along an expedient but ultimately tragic path: and part of our original sin is our original error, which yet paradoxically seems an absolute, inescapable necessity of our original existence.

The primal fault; our loneliness, our individual uncertainty, our need for love and our proclivity for hatred; with this we come into the world and with this we are ready and raw material for suspicion, fear, hatred, prejudice, and all un-charitableness. Racial differences, real but biologically by no means dangerous differences, provide yet one more occasion for stubborn stumbling, for pride, for suffering and inflicting pain. For every time we yield to prejudice, every time we insist upon our supreme distinction from other men, then, whether we know or acknowledge it or not, our guilty hand is reaching for a stone. Can it be that although in the Bible God reminded us that He had made us all from one mould, He has perhaps left it to us to discover just how difficult it is to live up to this, as to so many other truths?

Now as I speak as a very poor kind of Christian, the doubting, believing, ineffectual kind of Christian, such as most Christians are. I believe that God's own suffering, and God's own purpose, are inscrutable in this respect. I only know that when God Himself came as Christ into human society, He didn't last very long. For the standards which He proclaimed, and the suffering which He was prepared to endure, caught up with Him after only thirty-three years; and then, without condemning us, He let Himself be killed by us.

Is this then the message? That the only answer to cruelty, the only answer to prejudice, is in the open unprejudiced love in the heart of each one of us; a love which must be openly acknowledged, fearlessly followed through? It may seem strange that after an examination of the psychological founda-tions of something so universal, so indiscriminate, so recklessly justified, so stubbornly upheld, so irresponsibly loaded with misleading information, we should come back to the simple truth that only within the heart of each one of us lies the final solution. We must learn to love others as ourselves; unless we can do this, we not only doom others but are doomed ourselves. But if we can do this there is no problem of racial or any other kind of prejudice which need overwhelm our judgement.

Renunciation of Self-Centredness

If we can but renounce our innate determination to regard ourselves as unique and of supreme importance, with everything else going to the wall, then we can tackle this. But unless we are capable of this renunciation of self-centredness, then we cannot tackle it at all. Love and humility are the only answer to this problem and they must be calmly and vigorously maintained in the face of prejudice, in the face of indignation; of segregation, of all arguments, all the answers about what is good and what is sound, and what is practical for society and so forth; because these answers and arguments are based ultimately on fear, hatred, insecurity and the threat of being regarded as just like other men. Humility then and acceptance, are part of love: and love alone can pay the price for the abandonment of prejudice—and its natural outcome.

Negroes, Chinese, Arabs, Eskimos, Caucasians must be free to marry and be given in marriage. The diversity of human races which are simply a reflection of genetic flexibility, and of cultural and geographical diversity, must nevertheless not be segregated and kept apart but must be encouraged and enabled to unite. I believe this, and I put this forward as my personal answer, as a suggestion to this enormous problem.

The roots of prejudice are not in the actual fact of difference; or in the supposed superiority or inferiority of one race to another; persecution arises not primarily out of bitter situations, not out of frictions of human proximity or distrust, which varies by distance, but simply out of the will of living man to think more highly of himself and less highly of others than he ought to think. The essential feature is the inescapable self-centredness, separateness, and tragic personal pride of each individual one of us; whereby we do not love others as ourselves. If we can begin on that, we can begin at last to face and then, perhaps, one day finally to solve the problem.

CHAPTER SIX

THE BIOLOGY OF RACE

by

David R. Hughes, M.A., PH.D.

Dr D. R. Hughes is Professor of Anthropology in the University of Toronto, and was formerly University Demonstrator in Physical Anthropology at the University of Cambridge.

The Development of Hominids

The biology of race is encompassed by the study of hominid evolution and of human variability, and is the peculiar concern of the physical anthropologist and human biologist. The scientific discipline of human biology, into which physical anthropology has now grown, is competent to speak in objective terms about the biology of race, drawing observational data, not only from its own investigative sources, but also from numerous peripheral sciences such as human genetics, human physiology and bio-chemistry.

What is now known, from increasing fossil evidence, of the development of the hominids (i.e. creatures who, by various criteria, are commonly defined as men) suggests that there have been three major and successive evolutionary grades—the australopithecine grade, the pithecanthropine grade and the hominine grade. In terms of antiquity, contemporary dating techniques now suggest that the first grade was manifest about two million years ago, the second about half a million years ago, and the third about quarter of a million years ago. It is now becoming clear that overlap in spatial and temporal terms occurred between populations of early hominids representing the first and second grades, and also between those of the second and third grades. There are numbers of fossil hominids, therefore, of somewhat controversial taxonomy who might be regarded as being of intermediate grade, for human evolution is viewed as a continuous and continuing process.

The most marked physical difference between the three grades is in brain size, which is assessed for fossil man from estimates of cranial capacity. Here too, the impression is one of a gradual expansion through the three grades, with no abrupt divisions, although there is still uncertainty about the ranges of cranial capacity within the first and second grades as the populations involved are only represented so far by small samples. There is little reason to suppose that the three grades (the third being understood to include contemporary mankind) do not share elements of a common heritage.

In terms of taxonomy, the first grade is populated by one genus, *Australopithecus*, and the second and third by the genus *Homo*. Although there is still controversy, this represents the present consensus of informed opinion. The second grade is occupied by the species *Homo erectus*, and the third by *Homo sapiens*. Sub-specific differences do occur, and on this level we may choose to distinguish, for example, between Java Man and Pekin Man (both *Homo erectus*) or between Neanderthal Man and Cromagnon Man (both fossil representatives of *Homo sapiens*). There is now little argument in human biology that all of contemporary mankind falls within the one species *Homo sapiens*. The grossest differences between populations today, then, can at the most be only sub-specific ones. Our species, therefore, may be spoken of as polytypic, exhibiting a wide spectrum of variability (for example, in skin colour and hair colour). But each individual member of our species is genetically unique, the nearest correspondence in this regard being observed between identical twins.

So, despite the apparent uniformity of a character such as skin colour in a particular people, there exists, based on this uniqueness of the individual, a considerable range of variation for other characters or traits. Even the apparent uniformity of skin colour is illusory, as objective spectro-photometric methods of measuring skin pigmentation demonstrate a wide range of individual values in all population samples studied.

Innumerable examples of this uniqueness of the individual can be extracted from the observations of human biology. Dermatoglyphic studies, for example, demonstrate that no two persons have identical finger or toe prints. Nevertheless, if we study in this way successive random samples drawn from a particular population we find that they all exhibit a considerable degree of similarity in the totalled frequencies of the various fingerprint or toeprint patterns. In terms of the individual, then, there is variation; in terms of the population from which he comes, there is uniformity.

The Concept of "Race"

The human biologist is particularly careful when he uses the term "race" to make clear the context in which the word is being used and the value that he is awarding it. This is because experience has taught him that it is a term used somewhat loosely by others, and a term that is often used ambiguously in articles and books purporting to deal with what is sometimes called "racial anthropology". In the strictly taxonomic sense, there is no official recognition given to classificatory categories below the specific level, so in the formal terms of zoological nomenclature the term has no validity. Even today, in an age of supposed enlightenment and spreading education, there is much indiscriminate use of the term, as if its use conferred scientific respectability, when dealing with populations arbitrarily distinguished on a basis of language, political nationality, culture pattern or some somatic character such as skin pigmentation that is erroneously considered to divide up the world's peoples in some discrete fashion.

The sense in which the term "race" is understood by the majority of human biologists is to indicate a group of individuals marked out by some distinguishing characteristic or characteristics from the larger assembly of forms within their own species as the result of conditions imposed by isolation (with its concomitant endogamy). These conditions might be mutation or selection or both. Isolation might be imposed by oceanic or mountain barriers; it might be imposed by religious convictions or cultural conventions. Isolation therefore may be geographical or it may be social. Races, in this sense then, may be large or small, and they may be expected to be dynamic rather than static entities. When the evidence of prehistory is examined, however, the overwhelming impression regarding our own species, *Homo sapiens*, is one of restless migrations which have their continuation in the contemporary movements of the members of our species. *Homo sapiens* is now so numerous that it has been claimed that over half the total membership of the species since it evolved is alive today. In view of this history of specific mobility, many human biologists are doubtful whether any particular assembly of peoples or populations has been able to remain isolated long enough to be able to refine and perpetuate some unique constellation of characters setting it apart from the rest of mankind. Many are doubtful, too, in view of this mobility, whether the existing major populations of mankind were uniformly predominant in the past. Some human biologists would go farther and declare that discrete major races of mankind do not exist today and never existed in the past. Their argument depends greatly upon the observed clinal nature of much genetical variation within mankind, that is to say there are seldom abrupt boundaries between the incidences of certain characters in populations but only gradual and continuous changes in frequencies. Exceptions, when they occur, are usually caused by major geographic barriers, such as the Himalayas.

In scientific usage, then, the term "race" is largely a semantic convenience to refer to major populations or to small ones identified temporarily for the purposes of some empirical study by reference to an arbitrary number of criteria based upon the frequency of certain characters. Defined in this way, it will carry deliberately no connotations of unreasonable temporal extension back into prehistory. For the human biologist, then, the study of race is no longer an obsession with typological inquiry, a largely sterile approach, but a preoccupation with the effects upon our species of the forces of adaptation, selection, hybridization, migration, culture, prehistory and history.

Racial antipathies, although they cannot be justified or defended upon biological grounds, undoubtedly exist in the world today. The reasons for such antipathies must be sought for in the social, economic and cultural circumstances that permeate the life of any community. The legacy of an older physical anthropology, nurtured by mid-nineteenth century speculation about evolution, is still with us, and prejudiced men still seize upon its illusory premises in an attempt to prove the scientific bases of their own convictions. An example of this perversion of science is the past attempt by Nazi Germany to preach and impose a doctrine of racial hierarchy upon the populations of the world. Having purportedly identified major races, it is but a small step to seek to arrange them in some order of superiority and inferiority and to seek reasons for these disparities in terms of visible physical traits.

The history of these searches is a long one. The sacred books of India, for example, seek to explain and justify the distinctions considered proper between the various castes; early Chinese literature contains uncomplimentary references to those people not fortunate enough to have been born in the Middle Kingdom; a facility for racial discrimination is displayed in the wall paintings of dynastic Egypt at the tombs of the kings in Biban-el-Molouk. The relationships between victorious countries and vanquished ones, between masters and slaves, between kingdoms and colonies, have frequently been discriminatory ones. The attempts to find biological exculpation have been numerous and assiduous, but lack scientific validation.

Today, the word "race" is still commonly misused by many who may be precise enough in other respects. Thus one often encounters spoken or written references to the "French race", the "British race", or the "African race", when the intention is to indicate a linguistic, political or geographic grouping of peoples. Such a colloquial practice can be defended, of course, on the grounds of common usage, but the unfortunate corollary is that such misuse may give rise to illicit impressions of biological uniqueness and cohesion.

Genetics, Heredity and Human Variability

In its biological connotation, the study of race draws greatly upon the findings of the science of genetics. It owes a great deal, therefore, to the pioneer work of that thoughtful Christian, Gregor Mendel, sometime Abbot of Brünn. From his careful and patient experimentation, and from the timely rediscovery in 1900 of his laws of heredity, came the formulation of the scientific study of inheritance and the elucidation of the genetic basis of individuality. Mendel expounded the principle of particulate inheritance, and from this came subsequent developments culminating in the clarification of the mechanism of gene action and of gene change, or mutation. Much remains to be learned about the genetics of man, particularly regarding the interaction between environment and the genetic endowment of the individual.

It is now know that each human individual, with certain pathological exceptions, carries twenty-three pairs of chromosomes in the nuclei of each of his body's millions of cells. In the sex cells, however, there is a reduction process so that only one chromosome from each pair appears in each cell, instead of the usual paired complement. Thus a child will receive half its father's set of chromosomes and half its mother's. The genes may be regarded as being carried on these chromosomes. Every person has therefore a biological inheritance consisting of genes inherited directly from his parents. Notwithstanding the strong parental likenesses that sometimes persist, it follows that no child can ever be an exact genetical copy of only one of its parents. The totality of the genes on a person's chromosomes makes up the "genotype" of that person and represents his genetical uniqueness. Not all genes are of equal expressive power, so not all may manifest their presence in such a way as to be detectable to the naked eye. What the naked eye (or the microscope, for that matter) sees is a person's "phenotype", which is determined by those genes that are expressing themselves together with the visible effects of mediation from the environment. Thus, an obese man may be so from genetical factors predisposing him, although eating moderately, to put on weight, or from environmental factors such as habitual over-indulgence in food and drink, or from the interaction of both kinds of factors.

The totality of genes possessed by a human population is spoken of as the "gene pool" of that particular people. Populations may differ in the proportions of the various genes making up their pools. The human blood groups are good examples of characters whose inheritance is now understood fairly well.

Populations with different gene pools may differ in certain blood group gene frequencies. This has led some human biologists to write and speak of "microraces" defined by differences of this genetic kind. The frequencies of certain blood groups genes in the population of Wales, for example, are slightly different from those observed in southern England. It should be noted that it is not the unique possession of a certain blood group that distinguishes a population, but a difference, large or small, in the frequency of the genes responsible for a blood-group system.

A brief illustration drawn from the genetics of one of the blood group systems will be of assistance in demonstrating the workings of heredity in man. The ABO blood group system is a well-known one, and each person when typed proves to be of either blood group A, B, AB or O. This blood group is part of his phenotype. There are the following possibilities: blood group A, genotype *AA* or *AO*; group B, genotype *BB* or *BO*; group AB, genotype *AB*; group O, genotype *OO*. (Genes are distinguished here from groups by being italicised.) Genes *A* and *B* are of equal expressive power, but both are dominant over gene *O*. Thus a father with genotype *AO* (group A) and a mother of genotype *BO* (group B) can have a child of blood group A, B, AB or O, one gene coming from each parent, the possible genotypes that could arise being *AO*, *BO*, *AB*, and *OO*. These genes are transmitted within the male and female sex cells, and the selection of the actual pairs making up the genotype of the new child is essentially a completely random process, dependent upon the potential present in the genotypes of both parents.

Thus a calculation of the frequencies of genes *A*, *B* and *O* in samples of human populations often yields important indications of affinities between them, although it is uncertain how long such frequencies may be expected to have remained stable back in the past. There are, however, numerous other blood group systems of anthropological importance, two of the best known being the Rhesus system and the MNS system. Thus frequencies based upon a number of blood group systems can

D

afford greater confidence in the results of the comparisons of populations. In general, the results of such studies may be said to confirm what is already known regarding the distribution, dispersal and affinities of human populations. Energetic efforts are being made to extend this blood grouping technique to samples of bone from early man, but results so far are inconclusive.

It is thought that all physical characters in man are controlled to some extent by one or more pairs of genes. However, as has already been mentioned, it is difficult as yet to say how many genes are responsible for a character such as head length or stature, or in how far these are mediated by environmental factors such as climate, exercise or diet. Human variation falls broadly into two classes, discontinuous or qualitative, and continuous or quantitative. Discontinuous variation is thought to be controlled by a single or a few major gene pairs; continuous variation is thought to be controlled by the concerted action and interaction of numerous gene pairs. Thus a person is either of a particular blood group or he is not—this is qualitative variation; his height may fall between five feet and six feet, perhaps—this is quantitative variation. In general it is found that there is more variation within a sample for a particular character than there is between the average values for the character for two population samples.

The Influence of Natural Selection

Some knowledge of the principles of genetics is essential, therefore, to understand the nature of human variability and its inheritance. The mechanism for change within species, and the one encouraging the rise of sub-specific differences, is largely natural selection. The importance of this agency was emphasized by Charles Darwin in *The Origin of Species* over a hundred years ago. Through the effects of natural selection, then, populations of people undergo gradual change so that eventually descendants become less and less like their ancestors, considered phenotypically as well as genotypically. Thus, although populations of man can be traced back through the various evolutionary grades to common hominid ancestors, they will differ from these and they will differ in some contemporary respects from one another. As every human individual is unique, so in many ways every human population is unique, too. Natural selection involves adapting to the challenge of many environmental agencies, ranging from the food supply which may be scanty or plentiful, restricted in scope or very varied, to disease, a very potent agency for change, and one that favours the growth of immunity of one kind or another in succeeding and surviving generations.

The immeasurable complexity of human environments, and the interplay between factors making them up, however, means that inquiry has so far, as a matter of practical necessity, to be confined to attempts to define broad generalizations concerning the effects of, for example, hot climates and cold climates upon human populations. Thus variations in skin pigmentation have indubitable adaptive value, darker skins protecting their owners better than lighter ones in lands with long hours of strong daily sunshine. Similarly, body build appears to have become adapted in some populations today, the smaller and lighter peoples of the world tending to be found nearer to the Equator than the taller and heavier ones. The observed distribution of such variability is frequently complicated, though, by migrations of peoples, or by hybridization, so no more than broad generalizations can usually be made. It is often easier to point to examples of adaptation in animals lower than man in the evolutionary scale. It is true, however, that the study of differences between peoples in body size, body build, body proportions and skin pigmentation yield reasonably convincing evidence of adaptation in man to the various climatic extremes. The relevance of this so far as the biology of race is concerned is that such differences are frequently observed to transcend so-called racial boundaries. We learn, too, that there may be more than one possible human response to an environmental challenge. Any large region such as a continent will exhibit a considerable range of environments, and it is only to be expected that particular peoples may vary in their patterns of adaptive response. On every continent, and in every geo-graphically-defined race, there is a considerable range of variation in characters such as skin pigmentation, stature and head shape. Racial labels such as "White", "Black", "Yellow", "Caucasoid", "Negroid", "Mongoloid" and "Australoid" can convey nothing of this variability, and point to the futility of considering, for example, all the "black" peoples of the world as being of one race. To mention only one instance, the Tamils of South India are considered by many anthropologists to be members of the Caucasoid major race, yet in skin pig-mentation they are darker than many African Negroes.

If by races, then, we mean the current geographical distri-butions of the world's peoples, then it is becoming increasingly clear that it is difficult to draw up hard and fast distinctions between them. The traditional criteria of skin pigmentation or head shape are of little utility. Genetically-derived data emphasize the essentially clinal nature of much of this kind of human variability. Certain genetically-determined "markers" originally hailed as being precise indicators of racial affinities (for example, the "sickle-cell gene" or the "Diego antigen") upon further inquiry become of modified importance. We know very little of the origins of the skeletal variation that may be observed between certain populations; the fossil evidence is insufficient, so far, to suggest anything more than tentative estimates of fifty or forty thousand years ago for the beginning of sub-speciation of modern *Homo sapiens*. We still know little, then, of the stability of past populations of man, except for very recent times.

This leads some to think that a basis for distinguishing between peoples may be found in an examination of their cultural histories, it being considered that some past civiliza-tions were superior to others in this respect. This subject lies outside of the competence of the human biologist, but he would stress the falsity of attempts made in the past to relate achieve-ment with characters such as brain size and superior intel-ligence. There is no known correlation between brain size, usually estimated from cranial capacity and intelligence, however measured, cases of abnormal pathology being of course excluded. In a normal European population a figure of about 1,450 cubic centimetres is usually considered as the mean male capacity; individuals may vary 400 cubic centimetres each side of this average value without showing any significant increase or decrease in intelligence and intellectual ability. It would appear that brain size is partly a function of overall bodysize—women, for example, usually being some 200 cubic centimetres less than men in cranial capacity.

The Biological Significance of Miscegenation

There is finally the matter of hybridization or miscegenation in man, a process that was and is all-important from the aspect of modifying the composition of gene pools, and of modifying phenotypic variability. Many people have expressed concern regarding this human predilection, feeling that in some way it is reducing the fitness of our species.

To the human biologist, fitness in a population is best envisaged as being indicated, on the one hand, by persistence in an ever-changing environment, and on the other, by success (as evidenced by the totals of population in succeeding generations) in the exploitation of some particular environmental niche. These responses will depend, of course, upon the genetical structure of the population and upon its ability, if necessary, to adapt itself. Human hybrid populations, having intermediate gene frequencies and having intermediate phenotypical characters, might be expected to display intermediate fitness in either of the two parental environments. This will be restricted to the particular functions that the genes control and for which the characters are useful. The difficulty in verifying this for the human biologist is the lack of suitable and comprehensive studies for human populations.

There is a certain amount of experimental evidence from hybridized animals or plants, suggesting for example the phenomenon of heterosis, or hybrid vigour, but whether these findings can be used in connection with man is still largely undecided. At least one example is known where human hybridization might result in an unwanted decrease in fitness in the resultant intermediate population. Erythroblastosis foetalis or haemolytic disease of the new-born is a disability, sometimes fatal, that is a result of rhesus blood group incompatibility between mother and offspring. Some populations of mankind have a very low incidence of the rhesus negative genes, and therefore a very low incidence of this blood disease. Other populations have much higher incidences of the genes and of the disease. Hybridization between such populations, if carried out on a large enough scale, would obviously increase the likelihood of the disease in the intermediate population beyond that existing in the relatively unaffected parental stock. A similar situation will exist whenever two parental stocks concerned in miscegenation differ significantly in the incidence of other deleterious genes. It is a fortunate circumstance that such deleterious genes are usually rare in populations of man, except in small, isolated populations that may be consistently inbred.

Advances in medical technology, too, are only one example of how human culture is interposing barriers between man and harmful aspects of his environment, reducing what might previously have been serious hazards to the fitness of a population. A further reassurance comes from the view of some human biologists that all living races, however defined, spring from hybrid origins. In fact, new populations continue to evolve, such as the North American "Coloured" population, the "Cape Coloured" of South Africa, the "Ladino" of South America, and the "Hawaiian" population. Many other populations have changed the composition of their gene pools in historic times, for example the Eskimo of the Canadian Arctic and the Ainu of Northern Japan. Most unbiased observers agree that there has been no evidence of any obvious physical disadvantage resulting from such known human miscegenation, although its social consequences are sometimes unfortunate. The study of the inheritance of mental characteristics is complicated by lack of knowledge of the genetics of such attributes and by the tendency to value attributes that one's own society considers important.

It is possible to argue, however, that in any population of man, the fitness of the group will often be dependent upon the efforts of a few exceptionally gifted persons. Hybridization, implying the recombining of gene pools, increases the genetical potential of the resulting group, and increases the chances of outstanding individuals to emerge, although the opposite must also be said to be likely to occur at the other end of the scale of heritable abilities.

The evolutionary progress of man has been dependent upon his ability to transmit and exchange his genes with others of his species. Man is born into and dies within a social system; the genetical facts of his birth and death therefore work to change the gene frequencies of his population.

Professor Washburn, of the University of California at Berkeley, expressed the views of the human biologist very aptly some years ago when he said, speaking of man and race:

"We know of no society which has begun to realize the genetical potential of its members. We are the primitives living by antiquated customs in the midst of scientific progress. Races are products of the past. They are relics of times and conditions which have long ceased to exist."

We are fortunate in that man, of all creatures, is singularly educable; we have today, then, both opportunity and urgent reason for science and religion to work together in a common endeavour to preach and demonstrate the equality and unity of man within mankind.

CHAPTER SEVEN

THE CHRISTIAN VIEW OF INTERMARRIAGE

by

Roy S. Lee, M.A., B.LITT., D.PHIL.

The Reverend Roy Lee is a Church of England clergyman who is Chaplain of Nuffield College and St Catherine's College, Oxford. He is a theologian who has some personal experience of the problems about which he writes in this chapter.

The Significance of Colour

It would be false as well as foolish to maintain that in the Christian view a man's race or colour is unimportant. On the contrary, it is very important. It is certain to have entered deeply into his character and to have contributed much to the shaping of his personality. It is an essential part of him. It is the belief of a Christian that God values every individual as of infinite worth, and the Christian endeavours to do likewise, even if in fact he falls short of this ideal. He must value a man's race, therefore, just because it is part of the man and has helped to make him what he is. The Christian does not love man in the abstract; he loves his fellow men. That a man's race or colour is different from his own can never be a reason for despising or rejecting him; it is simply a feature of the man he is bound to love. On the same principle he does not love a man because he is white or brown or black; he loves him because he is a person, and his colour is valuable only because of the contribution it makes to his personality.

It follows from this that the Christian cannot hold difference in race or colour as in itself a barrier to marriage. When two persons marry they marry as persons and their race and colour come into question only as they affect the personalities of the couple and thereby make it difficult for them to attain the unity which is the ideal of marriage. But many factors other than race work against this unity, differences of religious affiliation, for instance, and inter-racial marriage differs from intra-racial only in the extent to which factors of race create problems of personal relationship. In other words there is no special problem of inter-racial marriage; there is only the problem of marriage. Christians do not take marriage lightly. They are not blind to its problems and what it demands of its partners, but they hold a view of it which society in general tends to regard as extreme and rigorous. In saying that inter-racial marriage is like any other marriage they are not denying its difficulties but only asking that these difficulties be understood in the right way, as problems of relationship.

My contribution to this symposium could well end at that point, but it may be useful to set down how one Christian, who has himself had personal experience of some of them, sees the problems which arise from inter-racial marriage. They involve the couple, their relatives and friends, and their children. Let us begin with the partners in the marriage.

When two people fall in love the attraction which brings them together involves many elements of a chemical, biological, psychological and spiritual kind. Any one of these may be exaggerated at the expense of others, but in the last resort it is a mystery why two particular persons fall in love with each other. What seems important is that the attraction should work at all levels. There should be physical attraction, probably based on unknown chemical factors, which may trigger off the biological urges to mating. These in turn flow into the psychological and spiritual. Of course the process may begin at any level but it is desirable that all should be involved.

It is not known whether racial differences provide any special attraction on the chemical and biological levels, but racial differences certainly enter into the psychological and spiritual levels of personality. They may in any given case strengthen or weaken the attraction between two people which falling in love implies, but they become highly significant after marriage has taken place.

The Unity of Marriage

Marriage, in the Christian view, demands growth into a unity, which is most obviously expressed in the union of bodies and the begetting of children, who are in the most real sense the union of the bodies of the husband and wife. This is one reason why the Marriage Service, in the Book of Common Prayer for instance, lays stress on the begetting of children as an essential aim of marriage. But much more is required for the unity of a marriage than this sexual and biological union. The two persons, with all that personality involves, have to grow into a relationship of sharing, mutual dependence and trust, so complete that the two function as a unit.

The unity of marriage cannot be likened to any other union of people. It is a unity hard to describe. Husband and wife do not become one person; they continue to function as separate individuals, and each may, even must, pursue interests widely divergent from those of the other. Yet they identify with each other so that each accepts and rejoices in the interest of the other and the divergences are an enrichment instead of a weakening of the unity. The partners complement and in some sense complete each other. True marriage means that each becomes part of the being of the other. This deep-seated identification with each other enables them to reach a common interest to which their separate interests become subordinated. Sometimes this may demand considerable sacrifices by one or the other, as for instance when the woman has to give up a professional career, but both must be ready to accept and accept willingly any such sacrifices required by the common interest. They must above all else support each other.

This is what happens in a successful marriage and this is the ideal in the Christian view of marriage. The fact that many marriages break down and many others fail to reach this degree of unity does not invalidate the ideal. It only points to the obvious fact that the unity of marriage does not happen automatically, either as a result of the marriage ceremony, or the experience of sexual union, or of the loving sentiments of the couple. Much effort and sacrifice, apart and together, is required of them before they can achieve and maintain the unity. They can only grow into it through the experiences of marriage. Before they are married they can only intend it in an abstract way, for they have to change to grow into it and the new way of thinking and living is impossible to them until they have grown into it.

Growth to Maturity

Such growth does not, I have said, come easily but requires effort and sacrifice before the full measure of identification is achieved. Many obstacles have to be overcome and these lie mainly within the personalities of the couple. Some of them are conscious, easily recognized from the beginning, but the difficult ones are unconscious and may destroy a marriage without ever coming to light. Given the willingness, and we can pre-suppose it in any marriage, two people can usually come to understanding and agreement about how to deal with manifest problems. Where they fail it is because there are underlying unconscious elements at work. Since the conscious level of the mind rests upon a broad base of unconscious material—memories, wishes, attitudes, feelings—we can expect difficulties derived from unconscious factors in all marriages, but they are liable to be especially severe in inter-racial ones, particularly if colour as well as race is involved.

People are not born ready-made. They grow up and the texture of their being is woven out of the experiences they undergo. They absorb the values, sentiments, habits, attitudes, outlook of the society in which they are reared, each person reflecting it according to the particular circumstances of his growth and to his own natural endowments. Colour and race are not something external or incidental to a man; they are himself. He does not become significantly aware of them unless he is faced with people of other race and colour. An alien in a strange society is made acutely conscious of his difference from the people with whom he is growing up, whereas in his own society he takes himself for granted and inevitably grows unconsciously into the pattern of that society.

Cultural Differences in Marriage

When two people of different cultures fall in love and marry they are not just two individuals conscious of and standing apart from the background of their lives: they are embodiments of their cultures and of their own individual histories. In striving towards the identification and full sharing which we have seen to be characteristic of a successful marriage it is not only the gap between the cultures from which they have come that has to be bridged. They can see the social

problems that are likely to arise and the difficulties of adjustment that one or both of them will have to face, and they can
take appropriate steps to deal with them. The real obstacle is
the gap between their personalities created by the long absorption of their respective cultures. They may well be blind to how
wide this gap really is, because the differences between them are
woven into the unconscious texture of their personalities.

The gap is less wide if both, though of different colour, have
grown up in the same general culture—black and white in the
United States, for instance—than it is between two who have
grown up in different societies—Britain and Ghana, let us say.
There are all kinds of complicating factors, education, religion,
profession, wealth, nationalism and so on. There is no general
rule to cover all cases. All we can say is that the couple carry
into their marriage the upbringing which has made them what
they are and the success of their marriage will demand sympathetic understanding of what each of them has hitherto
taken for granted. This will often be needed over what may seem
little things and in unsuspected areas of life—table manners,
personal courtesies, public behaviour, and so on. Inter-racial
marriage calls for greater adjustments and greater change of
outlook than does marriage between people of the same culture
and upbringing.

There is an extra difficulty involved when the partners come
from different countries. One of them, in most cases the wife,
has to leave the society and culture in which she was reared
and go to live in the native environment of her husband. She
will be unfamiliar with the conventions, manners, customs,
assumptions and values of the people among whom she will be
living. These are the things which make communication
between persons easy and which help mutual understanding on
a basis of equality. The wife will not only be a stranger in her
new setting, she will feel herself an awkward alien and be forced
into sharp awareness of her differences. She will be unable to
take herself for granted. She will not be allowed to do so. In
the new society in which she finds herself she is certain to
encounter prejudice against her or else an over-emphasized

friendliness which will make her aware that she is different.

On the other hand the husband will be in his own environment, not forced to think over all the things he has unconsciously assimilated, and he may not realize how great an effort of adjustment his wife will have to make and the restriction this puts upon her power to relax and express her personality easily and without conscious effort. There is a risk that he may be made too conscious of her alienness and begin unconsciously to resent that she is different from the people around them. As she in her loneliness will be turning to him for encouragement and support, any failure of this kind would create a barrier to the mutual identification which is essential to a successful and happy marriage.

Perhaps even more may be involved than the personal sympathy between husband and wife in this situation. She has to identify herself not only with her husband but with his work, his career and the milieu in which that is carried on. In other words she is called on to assimilate and not merely understand the new cultural setting in which she finds herself. She has to become a true member of her husband's society. She cannot change her colour or her race but she has to relinquish much of what made her what she is. This demands much of her and whether she can do it and remain essentially the same person with whom her husband fell in love depends upon his strength and understanding and her own character.

Encountering Racial Prejudice

I am for the moment dwelling upon the difficulties which may beset an inter-racial marriage. Before turning to what is to be set down on the other side there is a further one which should be considered. What has been said so far concerns the personalities which the couple bring to their marriage. But each lives in the context of friends and relations and the attitudes of these to the marriage can contribute much to its success or failure, and those attitudes are beyond the control of the couple. It often, perhaps usually, happens that the latter meet when one or both are away from home and therefore the parents and siblings at least see little or nothing of the other partner. They do not get the chance to discover him or her as a person, but inevitably tend to think of the unknown as a member of an alien race.

It is idle to pretend that race prejudice does not exist. It does and it runs deeply in most people. It can only be overcome by knowing the other as a person. When the opportunity for this is lacking the immediate relatives are likely to be hostile to the proposed marriage and sometimes even feel outraged by it. In any case they may not feel the same attraction to him or her, as the case may be. Where family or clan feeling is strong this imposes a further demand for sacrifice and can lead to the isolation from those who have been closest to one and who have contributed most to the shaping of his or her life. The ostracism is not likely to be so marked on the part of friends, because they are not so directly affected. There is no family pride involved with them. Their concern is more likely to be on the personal level. Nevertheless it is quite common for them to view an inter-racial marriage coldly.

I have been setting out some of the commonest difficulties which arise over inter-racial marriage. Let me repeat that analogous difficulties are likely to occur with any marriage. It is only that they are intensified when the partners are of different race and colour. This does not mean that they are insoluble. On the contrary inter-racial marriages start off with one great advantage, namely, that the couple know in advance that there are serious problems to be faced if the marriage is to be a success. This is not always the case in other marriages, for when two people are in love they are frequently confident that there is already perfect unity between them and they are blinded to the difficulties which inevitably lie before them.

When, however, they are of different race and colour they are always aware in advance that difficulties confront them. They may think that the difficulties will lie in the reactions of their friends and relations, and in the adjustments that the woman will have to make if she has to go to her husband's country, and in consequence may not realize the difficulties which lie in their own selves. Because they are in love they will be confident that their love is strong enough to overcome the difficulties. But at least they know their marriage will have its problems and they will go into it prepared in advance for the need to work on it. When the unforeseen problems arise they are more likely to face them openly than are other couples who have gone into marriage convinced that they have already attained perfect unity and only need to be married to complete it.

We can assume that the two love one another. What I have said implies that that love will express itself in deep trust so that they can freely discuss their problems without either giving the impression of disappointment in the marriage or with the other. This requires also sufficient intelligence and imagination to grasp the true nature of the problems as they arise. These qualities are needed in any marriage, so if the couple have them there is no reason why racial intermarriage should not be as successful as any other. Indeed it may be more successful, for the couple are prepared to face external obstacles and criticism, perhaps even ostracism, coming from their relatives and friends and from the social milieu in which they live. They will not make the easy assumption that there are no difficulties ahead. They expect them and this will make them in most cases more dependent on each other and more ready to come to that close personal identification which is the secret of any happy marriage.

Children of Interracial Marriages

There is a further matter of great importance to be considered. Children are the normal outcome of any marriage and when two people of different races marry they should give thought to the children they must expect to have and for whom they must hold themselves responsible. The parents go into their marriage fully aware of the prejudices which surround them. In facing these prejudices they have made a free choice. The children have no choice: they are brought into the world by their parents' decision. They belong to neither race and wherever they are they are certain to meet the racial prejudices which exist and which in some circles seem stronger towards half-breeds.

Children have not the inner strength which adults have developed to stand up against hostile criticism. They need to be loved and accepted by the group to which they belong. If they are not they lose confidence in themselves and become withdrawn or anti-social. Among their playmates they may not be made conscious of their difference, or that the difference in colour is of any great importance, for normally race prejudice is not present in young children. However, this absence cannot always be taken for granted, for children absorb the attitudes of their parents and without really understanding what is implied may call the children of mixed marriages by names which seem to mean that their descent is a disgrace.

On the whole, however, it is the treatment at the hands of adults, both overt and implicit, which tends to give these children the feeling that they are in some way inferior beings and makes them unduly conscious of their difference. Even people who are sympathetic to them and well meaning can foster this sense of being an alien in society and unaccepted, by their very efforts to console. All that such children need is to be taken for granted.

The sufferings of the children would be an almost insuperable argument against mixed marriages if there were not an even stronger factor to be taken into account to mitigate those sufferings and even turn them to good. The strongest influence upon children is the love they meet from their parents in a united family. They depend upon that love. It is that which gives them the unquestioned assurance that they are worth while, that they belong and have no need to question their right to exist.

If the husband and wife in spite of their difference manifestly accept, respect and love each other and treat their children in the same way they will imbue the latter with a sense of worth which will enable them to withstand the slights and intended

insults which they will meet. They may even gain strength
from these because the challenge makes them able to recognize
that they come out of a superficial view of what constitutes
worth in human beings and their own values will be deepened
in consequence. This of course does not necessarily happen, for
parents too often fail their children, and where they themselves
are under pressure, as will be the case in intermarriage, there is
always the risk that the children may be rendered vulnerable
to the treatment they encounter. But if the parents are able to
overcome their own difficulties and make a truly successful
marriage the children in their turn will be able to become true
persons in their own right and richer for the struggle they have
to make. Their achievement in this will in turn help to improve
the general attitude of society towards the mixing of races. In
the end it seems probable that prejudice about race and colour
will only be broken down by intermarriage on a large scale.

True as this may be it cannot be put forward as a justification
for any particular couple to marry. They may believe that their
marriage will ultimately prove a step in breaking down racial
prejudice, but this in itself is not a sufficient reason for marrying.
They will not be able to make their marriage a good one unless
they love one another. On their mutual love depends their
power to grow into the complete identity of interest which is the
mark of a true marriage, so their love must be the only reason
for wanting to marry.

We come back then to where we began. Inter-racial marriage
only differs from any other marriage because the gap between
husband and wife is likely to be wider to begin with in such a
marriage. But the same sort of effort is required of the two as in
all marriages. They at least have the initial advantage of
knowing before they marry that they must work hard at the
marriage. If they are both willing to do this no gap is too wide
to be bridged. The Christian view is that race and colour are
not important in themselves and therefore they do not constitute a barrier to inter-marriage in the abstract. But no
individual can become what he is apart from the circumstances
of his race and colour. There can be no Christian objection to

intermarriage. This does not blind us to the inevitable difficulties that such a marriage entails. The Christian simply asserts that these difficulties should be treated as questions of personal relationship, for to him the worth of persons is the essential matter.

CHAPTER EIGHT

THE BIBLICAL DOCTRINE OF RACE

by

Joost de Blank, M.A., D.D.

The Right Reverend Joost de Blank is a Church of England Canon of Westminster and Assistant Bishop of Southwark. He was formerly Bishop of Stepney and Archibishop of Cape Town from 1957 to 1963.

The Right Reverend Joost de Blank prepared this essay shortly before his death on 1st January 1968.

The Chosen Race

The movement of the Bible is from the particular to the universal. According to the Old Testament, God saves mankind from complete destruction by the selection of Noah, through whom He plans to create a new humanity. Later, God speaks to a man named Abram in Ur of the Chaldees, and promises that through his willing obedience all the nations of the earth shall be blessed. His name changed to Abraham, he is regarded as the father and begetter of the Hebrew people, which, as everyone who has dipped into the Bible knows, regards itself as God's chosen people.

No student at a theological college is left there long before he is confronted by what is technically known as "the scandal of particularity". This is a description of the strange way God has decided to bring about man's salvation. He does not write His Law in letters of gold across the sky for all men to read and to heed if they will. Rather He reveals Himself to a certain group of people so that through their self-forgetting service and obedience, the whole world may come to know and obey Him.

A great deal of the Bible is occupied with the hard fact that this does not work. People who are chosen very quickly forget the reason for their selection and begin to think that there must be something special about them. Conveniently they forget that God is their creator, and like to find in themselves certain qualities which, they are convinced, set them apart from the rest of men, and which account for their being picked by God as a people "peculiar to Himself".

There is a long list of failures but these are not allowed ultimately to wreck God's scheme. When the ten tribes of Israel disappear from history, the responsibility remains with Judah; and when most of Judah acts contrary to God's will, the prophets pin their hopes to a faithful remnant which may yet receive God's blessing and work His will in the world. The later chapters of Isaiah go so far as to suggest that this obedience may be concentrated in the faithfulness of one man, the suffering Servant, who stands either for an individual or for a dedicated minority.

Gradually there arises the hope of a Messiah, God's anointed one, who will be sent by God to recreate the chosen nation.

So far as Christians are concerned, this hope is fulfilled in the coming of Jesus Christ, through whose life and death and resurrection, a new humanity is brought into being. Those who receive salvation become members of Christ. This is a *new community* which unites all believers and is known as the Church of God. Again the same serving principle applies: the Church is not an end in itself but is the herald of the Kingdom of God which is the destiny for all mankind. Once more, the movement is from the particular to the general.

In contrast to the chosen people of the Old Covenant, the chosen people of the New is not dependent on national blood or an accident of birth. This was held to be true of Israel, though even here it has to be remembered that entry into full membership calls for the rite of circumcision. But for membership of the New Israel, which is the Church, there are neither national nor racial obstacles. It depends not on an accident of birth but on the miracle of rebirth, not on ethnic blood but on the redeeming Blood of Christ.

Into this new covenant all men are invited. There is no natural condition which makes one group more favoured than another. For all men can repent and put their faith in the Lord Jesus.

Apartheid, which is an Afrikaans word meaning separation, has become the dirty word of the twentieth century. And rightly so, for *apartheid* in South Africa means much more than this. It means *baasskap*, white domination, with all the misery it entails for the non-white population of that country.

Among the most valiant opponents of this pernicious outlook recently was Professor Keet, himself an Afrikaner, a Christian leader of wide repute who served for years as the Principal of the Stellenbosch Theological college, where many of the ministers of the largest of the Dutch Reformed Churches of South Africa are trained.

In 1953, speaking at an Inter-Church Conference in Pretoria, Dr Keet said: "There is only one *apartheid* known to Scripture, and that is separation from sin." No other criterion has any authority. Our relationship to our fellow men is based on the biblical assertion that we are all made in God's image. Which means that we share *one humanity*, with the same origin and the same potential.

One of the greatest dangers confronting the modern world is the "Chosen People" attitude, which believes that as a result of divine or evolutionary selection, one section of mankind is entitled to special privileges and authority over against any other. Nothing is farther from the message of the scriptural revelation which asseverates over and over again that when God chooses a people or an individual He chooses them, not for their own sakes or for any superior qualities they possess, but in order that He may use them to serve the rest of the world until all men find their essential one-ness in Him. The Israelites of the Old Testament doomed themselves to destruction when they began to take their selection for granted, even believing that this was due to some merit of their own. And we may be sadly certain that the same could happen to the Church, should it fail to respond first and foremost to its vocation to be a *caring* and *serving* fellowship, and it begin to think that it exists to promote its own continuance as an institution.

The three constantly recurring themes of the Bible are Creation, Covenant and Redemption, and each of these adds its quota to a common conviction about all human, including inter-racial, relationships.

The Concept of Creation

First, Creation. The Bible states quite confidently that man is made in the image of God. Modern cynics like to say that man makes God in the image of himself. Believers neither disregard the danger of such an exercise nor do they maintain that man has always been able to escape this particular temptation. Nevertheless, they assert that the formation of man is different from the rest of the world's creation. The statement that "God made man in His image" gives man an unique status. He is by nature a child of God, destined for God, and able to communicate with God.

On this premise, man's relationship to his fellow man is also established. His relationship to God is equivalent to mine. What I am in the sight of God, so is he. I am neither born with, nor on any grounds can I claim, a natural inborn superiority or domination.

In the scriptural record, the first two important questions put into the mouth of almighty God are these: "Man, where are you?" and, secondly, "Where is your brother?"

These two questions can never be separated. In our Lord's summary of the Law in the New Testament, He commands anyone who will be His disciple that he must love the Lord his God with all his heart and strength and mind and soul; and that he must love his neighbour as himself. These injunctions are the two sides of the same coin. They always go together and, for the believer, they can never be divorced. Cain may try to wriggle out of his responsibility for his brother's murder by asking plaintively: "Am I my brother's keeper?" But he is not allowed to say "no" in answer to his own question, and grim judgement falls upon him for his inhuman slaughter of Abel.

The racial problems of our day have been sadly exacerbated by men's refusal to accept their common humanity. As Lord Samuel once remarked ironically: "We are all brothers now, all Cains and Abels!"

This sense of the unity of the human race is common both to Judaism and Christianity as well as to the other great religions. Over the centuries it has become the heritage of civilized men everywhere. But the tragedy of history is that for all this man's essential brotherhood goes on being denied, often in word, all too frequently in deed, with the tragic result that the world falls apart into racial, ideological, national and economic fragments.

In the Acts of the Apostles, St Paul states the accepted view of both Old and New Testaments as he declares: "God has made of one blood all nations of men for to dwell on the face of the earth". (A.V.) This reads even more strongly in the translation given in the New English Bible: "God has made every race of men of one stock to inhabit the whole earth's surface" (Acts xvii. 26). It is in such a biblical conviction that man's conduct must be determined and performed.

The Concept of Covenant

A belief that the relationship between races should depend on the fundamental fact of man's essential unity speaks to all people taught in the humanities. In Holy Scripture, this belief begins with the doctrine of Creation. But it does not end there. It goes on to an acceptance of the further doctrine of Covenant, to which reference has already been made. This is a special relationship which exists between God and His own people, and is a faith shared by Jew and Christian alike, though the Christian refers to, first, the Old Covenant between God and Israel and, then, the New Covenant that has resulted from our Lord's life and death and resurrection.

It is no use closing our eyes to the unsavoury facts of history. Both Jews and Christians have all too often fallen below their own highest convictions. They have both found it easy to believe that they were chosen for their exceptional qualities, and not as instruments in God's hands to bring the whole world to a knowledge of His justice and His love. In becoming self-occupied, they have renounced their calling; they have been frozen in the particular instead of moving on to the universal.

The Gentile has often interpreted the Covenant-relationship of the Jews as a form of exclusiveness which has separated them from all other races to their own advantage and isolation. The Jew, with memories of all too many pogroms and persecutions, has seen a similar arrogance among Christians, who have regarded their faith not only as an excuse for molesting and ill-treating the Jews, but also as a justification for inhuman cruelties and betrayed confidences towards non-Christians in Muslim territories, in Mexico, North America and other parts of the world.

Wherever the idea of Covenant has led to actions of racial or spiritual superiority and domination, men have been false to the biblical foundation-articles of their existence.

So far as the Jew is concerned, this was put supremely well by Dr Leo Baeck in his famous book *The Essence of Judaism*, in which he wrote:

"Israel is chosen by God; therefore God is its judge. Israel is appointed by God to practise righteousness, and only if it does so can it and may it remain the chosen people; sin separates it from God, and forfeits its value. Its existence can be only a religious one, and it will be as it should be before God, or not at all.

"Out of this conviction there sprang the idea of the *world-historic vocation* of Israel, of its mission, and of its responsibility before God and to man. Election is conceived as a prophetic calling of the whole people. It becomes the belief in a mission which goes beyond Israel; Israel is chosen for the sake of others. All Israel is the messenger of the Lord, the Messiah, the servant of God, who is to guard religion for all lands and to radiate light to all nations. 'I the Lord have called thee in righteousness, and will hold thine hand, and will keep thee, and give thee for a covenant of the people, for a light of the nations; to open the blind eyes, to bring out the prisoners from the prison, and them that sit in darkness out of the prison house. . . .' Only a people which felt its own individuality in its soul could feel what its importance was to be for others" (Macmillan 1936, p. 61).

Dr Baeck wrote further:

"If Israel, as the bearer of religion, is the 'first-born son of God', this means that all nations are children of God, that they ought to be united with Israel in love for Him and in obedience to His commands. The tie of a common religious destiny unites all men . . ." (Ibid., p. 62).

To many people's surprise this line of conduct under the Old Covenant is not limited by race or natural relationship. It embraces the whole of mankind, and discrimination is forbidden. The book of Leviticus leaves us in no doubt: "You shall have one law for the sojourner and for the native; for I am the Lord your God" (Leviticus xxiv. 22). And this is stated, even more explicitly in the nineteenth chapter of Leviticus where these words appear: "When a stranger sojourns with you in your land, you shall not do him wrong. The stranger who sojourns with you shall be to you as the native among you, and you shall love him as yourself; for you were strangers in the land of Egypt: I am the Lord your God" (vv. 33 and 34).

The effect of the Covenant-relationship which Christians recognize, is closely related. To them, Jesus has come not to destroy the old with all its imperishable value but to fulfil it. Through the work of the cosmic Christ, Christians believe that all humanity is made one in Christ Jesus, and that in Him there is neither Jew nor Greek, neither bond nor free, neither male nor female, but a new creation which has been brought into being through the Divine redemption. Christ breaks down the middle wall of partition between Jew and Gentile. He is the reconciling agent in a divided world. In fact, He makes the Atonement, i.e. He effects the at-one-ment, through which men, made at one, secure that richness which is the fruit of a God-given unity in diversity.

The moment a person acknowledges the humanity of another, whatever the colour of his skin, his duty is clear. As a pointer, the First Epistle of John has these words: "If anyone says, 'I love God,' and hates his brother, he is a liar; for he who does not love his brother, whom he has seen, cannot love God whom he has not seen" (1 John iv. 20). The significance of this principle is spelt out when the writer says: "But if any one has the world's goods and sees his brother in need, yet closes his heart against him, how does God's love abide in him?" (1 John iii. 17).

In the First Epistle to Timothy, the author writes that "God is the Saviour of all men, especially of those who believe" (1 Timothy iv. 10). In the multi-coloured complexity of the Roman Empire, there was no place for racial discrimination. Even more, its very thought is alien to the whole spirit of the

Bible, and the new creation in Christ is the new patriotism which comes before any national or racial allegiance, and demands a Christian's primary loyalty.

Accepted earthly standards are reversed, as when our Lord tells His followers that henceforth greatness will be measured in terms of service and not in any material trappings. In the famous parable where Jesus speaks of the final judgement, He says of that day that God, "Will place the sheep at his right hand, but the goats at the left. Then the King will say to those at his right hand, 'Come, O blessed of my Father, inherit the kingdom prepared for you from the foundation of the world; for I was hungry and you gave me food, I was thirsty, and you gave me drink, I was a stranger, and you welcomed me, I was naked and you clothed me, I was sick and you visited me, I was in prison, and you came to me.' Then the righteous will answer him, 'Lord, when did we see thee hungry and feed thee, or thirsty and give thee drink? And when did we see thee a stranger, and welcome thee, or naked and clothed thee? And when did we see thee sick or in prison and visit thee?' and the King will answer them, 'Truly, I say to you, as you did it to one of the least of these my brethren, you did it to me'" (Matthew xxv. 33–40). We need to beware lest we fail to see the Christ in every man.

So far as the teaching of the Bible is concerned, there is absolutely no room for racial intolerance or colour discrimination in the Covenant-relationship between God and His people. Wherever today or in the past, any Jew or Christian has acquiesced in such discrimination, he has been false to his own standing within the Covenant of God, and his disobedience brings its own certain condemnation. Wherever believers have come to accept human relationships on a basis other than that of equal worth before God, they have managed to do this by a conscious (or it may be, on occasion, an unconscious) blinding of their eyes and stopping of their ears to the truths of the Faith which they profess.

The Concept of Redemption

For the Christian, the cardinal article of his faith is a belief in the Divine Redemption. He bases his salvation on the fact that the Lord Jesus Christ, the Second Person of the Godhead, became man and gave Himself for the redemption of mankind. He believes that God became man in Jesus Christ, that "the Word became flesh and dwelt among us" (John i. 14), which must mean that God has set His seal upon the whole of life, and that man in the totality of his being and environment comes within the sphere of the Divine redemption. Moreover, if the Incarnate Lord whom he worships took the simplest things of life, such as bread and wine, and oil and water, to convey most intimately the reality of His presence and His power, then there can be no doubt that physical man in his material situation is the object of God's saving love and action. It is well to remember that He who said that "man shall not live by bread alone" (Matthew iv. 4), also taught His disciples to pray, "Give us this day our daily bread" (Matthew vi. 11).

The Bible has little to say about "saving souls"; it has a great deal to say about "saving people". God's word to man is not addressed to his disembodied spirit but to man as he is, body, mind and spirit, his complete personality caught up in a chain of actual relationships, in a world where he both has to pray and to work for his daily bread, while recognizing as a child of God that his life is not restricted to this world only.

Surely this is one of the reasons why Christianity never took over the Greek belief in the immortality of the soul. Instead, every time he recites the creed, the believer asserts his faith in the resurrection of the body, which at the least means a belief in the enduring nature of the whole personality which, as far as this life is concerned, is enshrined in a capsule of flesh and blood through which alone it is recognizably singular and individual.

It is this stress on the material element in his faith which makes the Christian understand that the extent of his obedience is co-terminous with life itself. And from this physical involvement dare not, and would not, escape.

E

Of course, the attempt to escape and evade the consequences of such a Faith is made again and again. There are religious people, for example, who stress the Atonement at the expense of the Incarnation, and who profess a spiritual unity in Christ in the heavenlies, in the empyrean, sufficiently vague and distant and future, who yet reject unity in the life of everyday here and now.

There are those who are prepared to acknowledge a common faith in Christ, but who, nevertheless, refuse to shake hands with their neighbour, particularly if his is a hand of a different colour.

Let it be said categorically that wherever such a partial faith is proclaimed, it is not classic Christianity, it is not the historic Christian faith, it is not the Gospel of the Incarnation; and its advocates do irreparable harm to the cause of Christ as can be seen in the widespread disillusionment all over the globe. Our faith is that Christ died for all and every man is a brother for whom Christ died. Man's acceptance of salvation by repentance and faith is open to all without discrimination or differentiation.

The Bible maintains that "in the beginning God created the heavens and the earth" (Genesis i. 1). God's will for mankind has to be worked out in the stuff of this material world. There are Eastern religions in which man is called to ignore the world, to treat it as an illusion, and to work out his eternal destiny in self-annihilation and absorption in the Universal Soul. The Eastern mystic rejects the world in an heroic attempt to lose himself in the Eternal Reality; but those who live by the Bible know they are called to work for the establishment of God's kingdom in *this* world, though it extends far beyond.

Scriptural revelation sees the historic fulfilment of the human creation in "the universal kingdom of God embracing all humanity" (Leo Baeck). Man is commanded to be holy because God is holy; and for this to have any reality it has to be worked out in the social and ethical demands of ordinary life. In other words, man asks for no cloistered seclusion—he refuses any ivory-tower sanctity—as he gives himself to do God's will in all that makes up his existence both as an individual and in society.

Justice and Compassion

Thus in Creation, in Covenant, in Redemption, the nature and quality of man's relationships with his fellow man are clearly seen—and in a sense nothing more need be said.

But "in a sense" only. For there is one other apprehension of the nature and purpose of God which serves as the motive for Christian activity in the field of race relations. This is the statement repeated over and over again in Holy Scripture that the God whom mankind is called to worship is a God of justice and a God of compassion.

If we would be true to this conviction, we shall become passionate advocates of social justice and equally passionate exemplars of inclusive compassion. The two must not be treated as being wholly separate and distinct. In the Old Testament, God's infrangible justice is often interpreted in terms of mercy and benevolence. And so far as Christ's followers are concerned, their compassion must be directed not only to alleviating pain and misery but also in a struggle for justice in racial and all human affairs.

In the famous parable of the Good Samaritan told by Jesus, the despised Samaritan takes pity on the stricken Jew and does what he can to help him through his suffering and affliction. But his compassion need not end here, and today would almost certainly not end here. He might well initiate a campaign to ensure that in future the Jericho–Jerusalem road should be properly policed and controlled. Prevention is often better than cure.

As the good Samaritan so plainly indicates, national or racial differences are to have no place in a man's response to another's need. He helps because the other man is his neighbour, and this is all the reason he needs.

We no longer live in a country as small as the Holy Land from which most of our Bible came. The world is losing its narrow frontiers, and by rapid travel and communication is speedily becoming one people. In spite of die-hard resistance by the few, racial exclusiveness is a thing of the past, and more and more the earth's inhabitants are recognizing themselves as one family. But though to many it may be a disease theoretically, it is anything but theoretical in Southern Africa, in parts of the United States or in the immigrant concentrations of Britain. Christians have a pressing and urgent responsibility for the coloured people who are now a permanent element in this country's population. The history of Jewry in the western world shows both the wickedness and shortsightedness of encouraging the establishment of segregated ghettos, and of refusing non-whites equal rights and privileges as well as equal duties and responsibilities with the rest of the community. As with the Jews in the past, so now with Asians, West Indians and Africans, these people have much to give. We stifle their contribution at our peril and dangerously impoverish the future of our land.

If, as we believe, God is the Father of all men, we must maintain at all costs that our brotherhood is real. We are not a savage pack of Cains and Abels.

The New Jerusalem

In the twenty-first chapter of the Revelation of St John is recorded the vision of the new heaven and the new earth. In the new Jerusalem which is the consummation of Christ's redemption, we read: "By its light shall the nations walk; and the kings of the earth shall bring their glory into it . . . they shall bring into it the glory and the honour of the nations" (Revelation xxi. 24 and 26). *This is the final vision: the world at one; all differences that separate done away; but all diversities that enrich welcome and invited.*

To us in the last decades of the twentieth century it all seems hopelessly impossible; but this is not just a New Testament pipe-dream. This is the purpose of the whole scriptural revelation, and to this cause all believers give themselves without reserve or limitation.

One of the most puzzling facts about mankind for anthropologists and historians is the origin of language, and of different languages in different areas. No generally accepted scientific answer is yet available; but in the childhood of the human race, an early historian of the Hebrew people gave his own solution of the problem. The splitting up of nations and the multiplicity of languages came as a judgement on men's pride, when they believed themselves to be as good as God and started to build a tower to topple Him from His throne. Moderns may smile at the story of the Tower of Babel, but it is a valid attempt to explain man's national and racial divisions in religious terms.

For the Bible student, the Tower of Babel leads forward directly to its counterpart in the Day of Pentecost when the infant Church was empowered by the gift of God's Holy Spirit and Babel's ill consequences were undone. As in renewed courage the disciples proclaimed the Gospel of salvation, we read that all who were within earshot heard them speak in their own tongues "the mighty works of God" (Acts ii. 11). As a result many were converted, "and all who believed were together and had all things in common" (Acts ii. 44).

Scripturally, Pentecost is the answer to Babel. Only a community filled with the Spirit of God is adequate to bring harmony out of disharmony, to create a generous unity out of diversity. This is the harvest of the At-one-ment indeed; and in the racial problems of our time, this is the call to all churches and to all individuals.

O Lord, we pray Thee to send Thy Holy Spirit of Love into the hearts of all men everywhere; and begin in me, for Jesus' sake. Amen.

THE THEOLOGY OF RACE

by

Adrian Hastings, M.A., D.D.

The Reverend Adrian Hastings, one of the younger Roman Catholic theologians, has taught at Bukalasa Seminary, Uganda, and is now at Kipalapala Seminary, Tanzania, where he is organizing studies of Vatican II in the context of the African Church. He is a member of the Joint Anglican/Catholic Commission which first met in 1967 at Gazzada.

Divine Selection

"Truly I perceive that God shows no partiality"(Acts x.34).
That was the comment of the apostle Peter when, helped by a
special insight, he comprehended that the division of Gentile
from Jew had ceased to exist. The long years of the Old
Testament had been years of apparent partiality, of divine
selection: "I will establish my covenant between me and you
and your descendants" (Genesis xvii.7). There was Israel, the
society of those descendants, an originally racial unity, the
chosen people, and there was the rest, the Gentiles, the people
without. Certainly the books of the Old Testament have many
and increasing universalist breakthroughs. Even Abraham's
initial covenant was seen as somehow for the sake of the others:
"In you all the families of the earth shall be blessed" (Genesis
xii.3).

The coming of the Messiah, Isaiah clearly saw, would not
affect Israel alone; it would bring "light to the nations" and
in those last days the peoples would come on pilgrimage to
Jerusalem—a symbol of visible unity. Certainly there was no
trace of apartheid in the eschatological vision of Israel: "In
those days ten men from the nations of every tongue shall take
hold of the robe of a Jew, saying, 'Let us go with you, for we
have heard that God is with you' " (Zechariah viii. 23). And
then they will sit down together at a feast of racial unity:
"On this mountain the Lord of hosts will make for all peoples
a feast of fat things, a feast of wine on the lees, of fat things full
of marrow, of wine on the lees well refined" (Isaiah xxv. 6).
Eschatological unity, yet actual division. Concretely in the here-
and-now a sense of exclusiveness and of apartness remained
stronger than that of universality, of human togetherness. The
covenant of inclusion within the divine protection did somehow
involve for the time being the exclusion of others. God had
shown partiality.

But not now in the time of fulfilment, not "according to
God's purpose which he set forth in Christ as a plan for the

fullness of time to unite all things in him" (Ephesians i. 9).
Isaiah's age of eschatological racial unity has now arrived.
This final plan of God in Christ can admit no partiality, no
exclusion even for the time being. "One has died for all" (2
Corinthians v. 14). For all. And this new unity of men in the
community of salvation has got to be shown forth. For all. Like
Peter, Christians, theologians very much included, have always
found it difficult to take those words quite seriously, quite
au pied de la lettre. But the barriers of nation, race, language,
country are all down. To the ends of the earth must the good
news go. Christ is one. Man is one. God is one.

Time after time there has been a tendency to slip back to
a theology of selection and of exclusion. "We are God's chosen
few, all others must be damned" is a refrain coming back in one
form or another with painful regularity. It is not, of course,
necessarily a racialist attitude, though it is surprising how often
and how quickly it has taken on racial overtones.[1]

Upon the other side there is the vista of universality, so vast
that it can hardly be comprehended in all its pathways, but
maybe opening suddenly before one at a moment of unexpected
enlightenment. Peter at Caesarea after the roof-top vision;
Paul erupting under a sudden intensity of perception into the
heart of human and divine experience: "God has consigned *all*
men to disobedience that he may have mercy upon *all*. O the
depth of the riches and wisdom and knowledge of God! How
unsearchable are his judgements and how inscrutable his ways!"
(Romans xi. 32–33). John contemplating the heavenly city:
"Behold, a great multitude which no man could number, from
every nation, from all tribes and peoples and tongues, standing
before the throne" (Revelation vii. 9). Who could really have
fathomed how those long centuries of choice and exclusion and
separation were ephemeral, preparatory only to this fullness of
unity, ultimately inadequate as a revelation either of God or of
man? Instead the "wall of partition" (Ephesians ii. 14 A. V.) is
down, the wall "between us and them" (Acts xv. 9). Instead we

[1] The Spanish Inquisition's doctrine of *limpieza* provides an interesting
example.

have one and all received the gospel of peace—"peace to you who were far off and peace to those who were near"(Ephesians ii. 17). Go into all the world and preach the gospel to the whole of creation: the gospel of peace.

The Divisions of Mankind

The Bible begins with Adam and the genealogy of Jesus too is taken in Luke's gospel back to Adam, son of God (Luke iii. 38). Here again we have the basic concern for all mankind. It is that which descent from Adam signifies—unity of all men in nature and need. All exist in the image of God, all are subject to work and suffering, all die. Cousins in nature, all are called to be brothers in Christ: Parthians, Medes, Elamites, . . . the Roman centurion, the Ethiopian minister. One of the most evident implications of the New Testament is then the total unimportance of race. Racialism is just self-evidently non-Christian, even though time and again Christians have indeed become racialists—often by thinking themselves back from the New to a twisted version of the Old Testament situation. Is not the Faith Europe, and Europe Christendom? Have the natives of America souls? Is not Britain the true Israel? God's own people and God's own land—God has chosen *us*, has given *us* this land, has made *them* different, hewers of wood, drawers of water.

Today the psychological division between "us" and "them" may often take, in the world at large, a more manifestly racial character than in the past. But it often tended that way: English and foreigners; Greeks and barbarians; Aryans and Jews; White and coloured. The building up of a situation of this kind and its segregationalist responses is all too characteristic of human society, but the Gospel has its response: a more explicit response than it has for almost any other social problem, and that just because the Church had to face such a situation—although one couched in particularly theological terms—right from the beginning. Despite hesitations countenanced by authority and deviationist groups with their very apartheid line—they refused to eat with the Gentiles and *separated* themselves (cf. Galatians ii. 12)—the Church's considered response was uncompromising: "God shows no partiality". The wall is down between "us and them".

Christian Universalism

Thus the Christian Church by the most striking facts of her mission and her earliest crisis in self-awareness has universalism built into her. The medieval tradition, which turned the wise men of the Epiphany—the very first Gentiles to worship Christ—into three kings, black, white and brown, expressed in its simple, popular, grass-roots way, the essential equality of men and of race in the light of Christ, which is something utterly to be taken for granted within the Church. She has always accepted her mission as one to all nations and has never admitted racial differences as a barrier to the Christian or human community. But only since the sixteenth century has she been faced with situations of continuous inter-racial contact on a large scale. It must be admitted that the result was in many ways not encouraging. Massacres of Indians, the organized slave trade, even the denial that these were really men at all. But the Church's voice did not hesitate. Not only champions like Bartholomew de Las Casas but the Pope himself spoke out with clarity: "The Indians, though still not received into the bosom of the Church, must not be deprived of their freedom or possessions, *for they are men*" (Paul III in 1537). It was the position of the great theologian of natural law, Francisco de Vitoria: natural rights belong to men because they are men, members of a single universal society. They admit of no racial distinction.

Rome's first "Vicar Apostolic" for Africa was a young Congolese, Prince Henry, consecrated bishop in 1518. Likewise the first vicar apostolic in India was a Brahman convert, Mathew de Castro, appointed in 1637. These were fine gestures, the instinctive movements of the Christian mind. They did, alas, remain little more. Further African and Indian bishops were not appointed in the Catholic Church until the twentieth century. The official position of the Church was one thing, the pragmatic attitudes and prejudices of most Christians anothet, and in practice the latter widely prevailed. Racial discrimination, even of a blatant kind, has been a notable feature of Christian life in many places in modern times—a discrimination which has penetrated even within churches and ecclesiastical institutions of all kinds. It is not the function of this article to study history, neither to excuse, nor to blame. Certainly in this matter, as in many others, we have sinned and need to admit it without circumlocution. Today the World Council of Churches, the Popes and the Vatican Council have all expressly condemned racial discrimination and that is certainly sincerely endorsed by the great majority of convinced Christians.

"The Church rejects, as foreign to the mind of Christ, any discrimination against men or harassment of them because of their race, colour, condition of life or religion" (Vatican II, 1965). "When we are given Christian insight the whole pattern of racial discrimination is seen as an unutterable offence against God, to be endured no longer, so that the very stones cry out" (W. C. C., Evanston 1954).

Life and property, all the exigencies of the human condition, fellowship with other men, the highest things and the lowest, the grace of God, the communion of the Church—all these things are offered to men without exception because they are men united in the solidarity of their common divine image, their common human parentage, their common redemption.

The Sacrament of Unity

That is the witness of the Christian Church and it always will be so. There can be no walls of separation. The Church does not teach a doctrine of invisible and spiritual things alone. On the contrary, she witnesses to the Incarnation—to God being with us. We saw him and touched him and ate and drank with him. Christians are the disciples of Jesus of Nazareth, those of his company who ate and drank together in fellowship and must still continue to do so. This living, human, physical being-together is the sign and sacrament of all she teaches and means. She cannot teach a spiritual unity and admit a physical separation. She does not even start with the spiritual unity; she started with the physical togetherness of a common board, supper with the Lord.

In the fine words of St Cyprian, repeated and stressed by the Vatican Council (e.g. in the Constitution on the Church, no. 9 and the Liturgy constitution, no. 26), the Church is the "sacrament of unity". A sacrament is a visible signpost, a credible manifestation, a showing forth in place and time such as men can understand. And this unity is a human one, a unity of men, of the men whom the Lord loves, of all men. To deny the spiritual unity and equality of men is utterly to deny the Bible; while to deny that this unity is and must be manifest in the visible Church, to admit apartness in the visible Church though not in the Spirit, would be equally to deny the Incarnation, that the Son of God lived among men, his Church a fellowship of men on earth, an eating and drinking society, a physical cum spiritual communion.

The basic physical element linking the initial company of Christians has always to continue. The Eucharist supper is the permanent centre and cause-of-being of the Church. Do *this* as a memorial of me. Eat, drink, together. We are one body for we share in the one bread. The absolute heart and essence of Christian living is the negation of apartheid: not uniform belief in the existence of God, but common drinking from a shared cup—the sacrament of unity. It is the unity of men as men in their very animality, and that is made the sign of the union of the spirit. The most earthly communion, the sign of the most divine: the bread we bless and break and eat together is it not a sharing in the body of Christ?

It is a sign with meaning. It really implies unity with God and unity among men. To eat together in church and to remain on principle apart in the seven-day-a-week life whose meaning has to be signed in the Sunday Eucharist would be utter nonsense.

It would make of it an empty sign, a farce. Far better not to go to church at all than to participate in that contradiction-in-terms a segregated eucharist or even in a eucharist for the segregated.

The Church of the Word made flesh is for all men, Jew and Greek, Roman and Ethiopian, and its membership involves physical fellowship. The life and unity she offers cannot just be a subject for belief, it must be lived, and lived in the flesh. Otherwise the Church is not the Church.

Man matters, and the universal brotherhood of man; race does not. That is not only a judgement of philosophical conviction or religious faith. When one has lived for years with people of another race, worked and played and argued and disagreed with them, when one has read together Antigone and Hamlet and St Joan, and shared their struggles and triumphs and emotional crises, and shared one's own with them, then one knows indeed with the conviction of the deepest human experience that men are one, and differences of race slip away into the fringes of insignificance. The death of Socrates is no more mine than theirs. It belongs to all whose humanity is sufficient to share in it and the experience of this joins us together inseparably as men, just as communicating in a common eucharist presenting the death of Jesus Christ joins us utterly as Christians.

The Diversity of Race

Is there nothing positive to say, then, of race? Is it simply to be dismissed as a false premise for segregation? That can hardly be so. The mystery of human experience is continually one both of unity and of diversity. When we speak of the first Adam, the historically first being who had a human destiny, and our common unity in him, we speak of a unity of poverty, of possibility, of what can become. When we speak of the second Adam and the uniting of all things in him who is Omega, we speak instead of a unity of fullness, of realization, of varied development. The unity of the last times is one of harvest, good measure pressed down and flowing over. Between one and the

other there must have been a vast multiplication of diversity—
the growing up of humanity, a growing up which involves too a
growing apart. The diversity of mankind, the non-uniformity,
is as significant as its unity; regimentation as criminal as enforced separation. Man must be man, not just *in globo*, but in
the development of his individual nature and personality. Each
is other, and this otherness penetrates all through us, all through
the complex of the spiritual and the material that is a human
being. We cannot be other in the spirit, but utterly uniform in
the flesh. For we are enfleshed spirit, rational animals. Just as
the unity of fellowship cannot be one of the spirit alone but must
be incarnated in physical life, so must our diversity—variety
in mind, but variety too in our very animality.

The range of physical variety in mankind is the essential
manifestation of this aspect of the human condition. The different features of the members of a single family, the similarities,
the strange combinations, the seemingly endless variety even
within the range of a particular type of human physique;
the slightly wider differences, at the national or regional level,
the blond Scandinavian, the black Spaniard; then the full
racial contrasts, deeper physical variations between the historically more distant branches of the human family; and always
within each group an equal range of personal diversification:
all this is the physical expression of the innate vocation of man
to be himself, to be sacramentally different and recognizable
from his fellows.

Race shows man as truly animal. We have no reason to be
ashamed of this. Just as there are different breeds of dogs,
so are there different breeds of men. We demonstrate our
collegiality with the animal world by being ourselves racially
diverse. All animal groups have this diversity within the species,
and if man is truly a "rational animal" then mankind must
share in a pattern of physical diversity relating to lineage
groups. "Man" in fact cannot be understood without "race"—
at least unless we believe in a neoplatonic soul-man. If man is
body too, if he is animal, then he is racial. This is by no means
his most significant characteristic but it is truly and necessarily

part of him. The having of race is not an extra, over and above a full anthropology, it is implied in a sound anthropology.

Indeed the various racial characteristics, certainly related in one way or another with the climate and physical pressures of different parts of the world, precisely express our individual human entity as being truly a participation in the physical cosmos, an "existence-in-the-world": part of the world, not just somewhat awkwardly placed here in a vale of tears to pass the span of our mortal existence, but truly growing and belonging here, being moulded and varied according to the pressures of wind and rain and sun, just like brother dog and brother horse.

But the enormously much greater complexity of variety in human features represents the enormously much greater richness of the human vocation. Like the animals, we express ourselves in physical features moulded by the forces of biology and geography working over the generations, but moulded too by personal character and experience, by work, by knowledge, by love. The physical diversity of men, from the bones to the twist of the lip, is the sacrament of human existence: the visible expression of intelligent beings fully participating in a material and animal world.

The Concept of the "Natural"

The fact of race is then to be recognized as, in a way, the typical manifestation of our created existence being a fully-of-this-world existence, and to be ashamed of it or to want to ignore it is really the expression of a manichaean or pseudo-platonist view of man as spirit alone, somehow contaminated by being subject to the conditions of physical animality.

We accept it: race is part of being man. Having recognized this we can see the danger arising of a false conclusion, the type of conclusion often drawn and somehow justifying racial segregation. Race is part of man, we say. It is then part of the natural order, God's plan for the world. Now modern conditions are mixing the races; they are producing inter-racial marriages, inter-racial societies. This development is confusing God's plan. On the contrary the natural order must be maintained: the races must be held apart. Apartheid is then a policy of human co-operation with the natural law of God.

A conclusion of this kind results from grave over-simplifications concerning the social consequences of a physical condition, the moral objectivization of a particular historical state of man, and indeed the whole conception of "being natural".

When we say that having race is part of the nature of man, we are talking about a physical condition not a social or cultural one. Historically the division of races has in fact corresponded to some extent with geographical and cultural divisions. That correspondence was natural too—using "natural" in a rather different sense: that is to say it was suitably characteristic of a certain not very evolved state of human society. Thus it is natural to use ones legs to move from one place to another, yet using a car is also natural; it follows from the whole nature of man—not only a two-legged animal but also an intelligent being, one able to adapt other material things and circumstances to satisfying his needs.

Again, it is "natural" to be of a race, but it is equally "natural" to be able to marry someone of another race. Such observations indicate one aspect or another of our being, they do not evidently imply one or another overall line of conduct. A half-caste is as "natural" as someone of pure race. A study of these things throws light on what we are, but it cannot create an imperative to maintain a particular condition.

The trouble here, as in so many fields, is to identify the "natural" (with a consequential moral law) with the historically prior condition, or with what is guessed to have been the historically prior condition. There is always a strong temptation to do this—to think of the natural as the primitive rather than as the condition which best expresses the inherent potentialities of such and such a being. One is Hobbes' state of nature, the other Aristotle's. For the latter, nature is to be found in the end. Man is a social being and both in himself and in society he can only express himself, he can only fully be himself, across a process of evolution, of the growth of human consciousness and human skills within a developing society. Man, segregated in his racial group and knowing only his own language, controlled in his life by the physical elements, using a few implements upon which he has imprinted his own character only very faintly, is man unevolved, largely unaware of himself, near the start of his providential pilgrimage.

On the other hand man who is the master of a mass of techniques which he has drawn out of the inter-action of his own intelligence and the world about him, who can share fellowship with men of origin far from his own, this "modern man" (full of dangers certainly—of possibilities for evil and cruelty and the final disaster of de-humanized enslavement to the very things he has created as means for humanization) is nevertheless—so long as he can remain equal to his condition—more natural than the other. He is living in a condition which he himself has made through activity natural to him, not in a condition in which he is simply found.

A healthy human society cannot but evolve, and in evolving it cannot but push outwards, link itself with other societies, grow with them into one, share and communicate and overflow: and this at every level of religion and philosophy and law and language and commerce and race. Man must mix and share, Mercians with Wessex men, French with English, European with African. The exigencies of human life and society necessitate it. Contact of course occasions conflicts, the building up of group rivalries, the fear of one's own identity being endangered. But the process is a continuous and inevitable one within human history and it is a condition for the "naturalization" of man, the achievement of a full humanity.

The category "natural to man" has as its absolute the still unknown end, but concretely its significance is then within a process of becoming; it cannot be validly assessed as an unchanging norm. Its understanding and application involve an historical context. In the year 10000 B.C. a thousand things, which we see as fully natural, even "natural rights", would have seemed infallibly unnatural and quite preposterous and would indeed have been quite unnatural to man then—totally un-related to his being and to his assessment of himself within the historical and social context that man was then in.

A World-Society of the Redeemed

The process historical man is within, or perhaps better the process which he is—despite regressions and sidesteps and pauses—producing out of himself, out of his needs and urges and aptitudes, is one growing together, not in absolute uniformity, but in a complex inter-dependent diversity. Historically the type of diversity based upon "separate development" and a rather low degree of external influence, which was character-istic of an early stage of human society, is everywhere giving way to a diversity of continuous inter-penetration. This is shown as inevitable by a study of the history of human society as we know it, but it can equally be seen to be demanded by a study of man as a social being, requiring as he grows in competence a society of ever increasing dimensions. Developed man cannot *not* live within a world society. This is called for too by the nature of Christianity, of the realized participation of all humanity in the New Adam and within the Church. From the very earliest times she has been entitled "Catholic"; *Catholic Church* means "World Assembly" and men cannot be assembled within the ecclesial fellowship if they are humanly and socially sundered. The Church is the salt and the ideal and the "so-much-more-beyond" of human society, not its antithesis.

Now the human quality of race must be seen within this whole vista of man-in-evolution, on pilgrimage. As a part of our nature, it is not to be torn apart and treated differently from the rest of how we are. Moreover since flesh must serve spirit, and this is as such so utterly characteristic of the flesh, of being animals, it has above all to serve the spiritual kingdom, the full advance of mankind in unity and truth, not be set apart as an object of adoration or of fear or of division.

Racially separate communities were characteristic of a rather unevolved pattern of human society. They are incompatible with a highly articulated and extended one. Today human society requires inter-personal and inter-group contact on a vast scale—at the level of mind and research, of commerce, of eating together, of race, of love. We meet as men fully, not as minds only or as a market for consumer goods. In the process of historical evolution in which we share, we have reached today the building of a single world society not in theory but in fact. We see this as demanded both by the facts of the contemporary situation—demographic, educational, economic, political—and by a full conception of what man is. But building a world society of man necessarily means building an inter-racial society, just because as we have seen, man is a racial being. To be fully man today, sharing in the "natural" condition for contemporary man, means then to share—and willingly—in inter-racial society.

As a member of the Church one's vocation in this age is still more wonderful. For the Church—truly the people of God—is herself too an "in-this-world" reality, her historical being and the temporal fulfilment of her God-given vocation is controlled by the historical condition of human society. She transforms the world, but also she grows within it. She is the Catholic fellowship, by her calling the world society of redeemed men, but she could not be this in act, in an achieved way, when there could not be a world society. The present historical condition of humanity is really making it possible for the first time for the Church to be herself: not merely to have members of many lands and races, but truly to be a fellowship, a living communion, of all nations—the sacrament of unity, that is a fully visible and manifest sign of a fellowship of love without bars and discriminations.

As racial characteristics are the most visible sign of difference and division within mankind and today present psychologically the greatest cause of separation and conflict, so it is intrinsically required that if the Church is to be a worldwide signpost of divine and human unity and that effectively for today, then she should above all be seen as an inter-racial fellowship. Only as such can she be credibly the great "sacrament of unity" in the twentieth century. Moreover as the local church is the microcosm of the universal Church, truly manifesting the character of the latter, so it is positively required that in an inter-racial area the local church too appear as an inter-racial communion, sacrament of unity for these men here. Failure to do this is failure to be the Church.

One God, one Lord, one Spirit, one destiny, yes but one flesh too: one incarnate Lord, and so one physical fellowship, one eating and drinking together. We who are many and diverse in skin and hair and jaw are one body, for we all partake of one bread.

CHAPTER TEN

A LOOK AT BRITAIN

Part I by An Indian Immigrant

Part II by A West Indian Social Worker

Part III by An African Student

By an Indian Immigrant

Images of Britain

The Indian very rarely looks on Britain as the "Mother Country", as West Indians are said to do, nor does he think of it particularly as a Christian country. He believes that Britain is a just and democratic society where through his own efforts he can carve out a happy future for himself and his family.

It may sound naïve but this assumption is indirectly the result of 300 years of British rule in India. The men who came to rule India behaved in public (Indians knew little of their private lives) as men of integrity, impartial in their attitude and dispensing justice without fear or favour. It was natural enough for the Indian to assume that the British nation as a whole possessed the characteristics of honesty and integrity displayed by its chosen representatives to the Indian public.

This feeling still persists in India today, and most Indians expect that they will be treated with respect and fairness when they come to Britain. The skilled immigrant believes that he will be treated on merit in contrast to the treatment he gets in India, where he has to fight against corruption and jobbery if he is to succeed in life. The unskilled immigrant is trying to get away from poverty, misery and frustration. He sees in Britain a highly industrialized society where jobs are plentiful, wages are good and promotion is on merit.

Encountering Prejudice

The Indian, I should mention, is not unused to discrimination. It exists in India even today, but being based on caste and creed it has become an accepted feature of Indian life and the Indian is apt to take it for granted. Colour prejudice, on the other hand, is something that the Indian does not know about. He meets it for the first time when he comes to Britain and finds himself treated as something inferior because of the colour of his skin.

Prejudice in Britain is not often practised openly, but it does not take long for the Indian immigrant to realize that he is unwelcome. This is brought home to him very subtly in a variety of ways, especially in the fields of work and housing. Well-qualified and skilled Indians have often found that they do not get the better paid jobs. It is obviously difficult to collect evidence that a man is rejected because of his colour, but sometimes the flimsiest of excuses are offered, or even none at all: just a polite rejection. Very few people in Britain realize the agony the immigrants undergo in their search for work. The hurt and the rebuffs they meet are an affront to their human dignity. Yet few people care because these persons are coloured, because they "don't belong here".

The unskilled immigrants have an additional handicap in their lack of fluent English. After their experience in India they are prepared to accept any job, no matter how menial, upon their arrival in Britain. The difficulty is in moving up from the lowest rung of the ladder when neither employers nor trades union leaders have much interest in seeing this happen. Not much effort is made to induct these immigrants into the British way of life.

Working conditions and housing, about which much more could be said, are the two biggest factors militating against the Indian immigrant. However, his integration into British society is made even more difficult because of the ludicrous misconceptions held by the British about the Indians. Very often they do not distinguish between the West Indians, Indians and Africans, but prefer to lump them together as "coloureds". It is not surprising that real friendships between members of the two races occur very rarely. Most of the British people do not take the trouble to learn the true facts about the habits and customs of the Indians. Paradoxically, the worst offenders in this respect are the middle class, supposed to be educated to a higher standard and capable of logical thought. It is these people more than anybody else who actively support discrimination. Advanced educationally and technologically, possessing an enviable democratic system and a comfortable standard of living—the British nation with all these blessings is not yet mature enough to face up to and seriously tackle the canker of prejudice and discrimination in the heart of its society. This apathy is the bitterest blow to Indians and is responsible for some of them becoming racially prejudiced against the British. They feel they are fighting a losing battle in their campaign for equal rights.

Christians Not Blameless

The saddest aspect of this situation, from the view-point of an Indian Christian, is that in Britain even Christians are guilty of the charge of actively practising discrimination. It would be reasonable to assume that as Christ's followers they would realize that any unfair treatment of immigrants was their concern. But how many Christians bother about these things? It is impossible to distinguish in Britain between a Christian and a non-Christian by his behaviour. Where the coloured immigrant is concerned they all behave alike.

This charge may sound too strong, but this is how it appears to the disillusioned immigrant. Christ's teachings embody those principles which, accepted as a way of life by his followers, would ensure the establishment of a just society on earth. "Love your neighbour" is so fundamental to Christianity, yet what is the attitude of Christians in Britain today? The commandments of God are accepted in so far as they suit individual tastes and preferences and those which appear unreasonable or unsuitable are rejected in favour of greed and selfishness. Christianity as a way of life seems virtually non-existent, at least not the full-blooded commitment that distinguishes good Christians in India.

It is easy to blame the leaders of the Christian churches in Britain for failing to give a firm lead to their flock. They have been far too content to follow public opinion rather than trying to change it. The Catholic Church is no exception, in fact it has been extremely timid in its denunciation of discrimination and up to date has done less than other Christian churches. In all churches, however, attempts to awaken social consciences have been sunk by the dead weight of apathy and indifference on the part of the lay body of the Church.

If Christianity is to be seen as meaningful by Indian immigrants, who may have had little previous contact with Christians, one thing above all is necessary. Christians must realize that the denial of equal treatment to human beings who happen to possess darker pigmentation is not only an affront to man but more so to the Creator who made us all.

PART II

By a West Indian Social Worker

Immigration from the New Commonwealth

Few developments in post-war British history appear to have attracted so much concern and evoked so much emotion as the fact of immigration from the newer Commonwealth countries. Migration in one form or another is not new to the people of this country. The history of what was Empire and is now Commonwealth, and indeed of other countries such as the United States of America, is the story of the movement of British people in substantial numbers to other parts of the world— a movement which is by no means at a standstill today.

Similarly, much of modern British society is the product of the movement of peoples from other countries to Britain. The main reason for anxiety appears to be the fact that whereas British people have always gone to live in America, Australia, Canada, New Zealand, Asia, Africa and the West Indies, and the people coming to Britain for settlement prior to 1948— whether from Europe (including Ireland) or elsewhere—were of similar colour and hair forms to the population here, the greater number of people coming to live and work here since

1948 have been of African or Asian descent—coloured. The largest single group are Jamaicans—perhaps 250,000 or more (including those born here of Jamaican parentage)—no one is very sure.

In the main, Jamaicans have been sufficiently naïve to have thought both at home and immediately after arrival here, that Britain, the heart of a multi-racial Commonwealth, would have welcomed their presence as a practical demonstration of the true meaning of multi-racialism. But this opportunity of building a homogeneous society with the aid of people from whom the country as a Colonial Power drew its wealth and prestige, was pretty well rejected—at least until 1965 when official policy started planning for effective measures to improve race relations.

The Background of Jamaican Immigrants

In discussing the reasons for the anticipations and aspirations of the Jamaican, we should examine one fact with which contemporary Britain ought to be *au fait*—the docking of the *Empire Windrush* at Liverpool in 1948 with the first large batch of immigrants from Jamaica. They were none other than people who had spent a long time during the previous seven or eight years in this country either in the armed services or in munition factories. It is not important here to discuss the reasons for their returning to Britain rather than remaining in their own country. These are too well known. What is more important is to appreciate that this was a group of Jamaicans who previously had come 5,000 miles away from their native land to be with the British people through peril, disaster and triumph. In so doing they had found friendship and comradeship, shared in a spirit of community, and in some instances had left behind their friends and relatives who had married local people and were raising families here. Equally important is the fact that the country needed no less in 1948, and subsequently, the services which the Jamaicans offered during 1939–45 and had come back to offer. They offered their services now, not out of the generosity of their hearts, but for the same reasons which still motivate the Englishman to emigrate to Australia, New Zealand, America, Africa and the West Indies.

The participation in the war effort, and the return of Jamaicans to Britain, were a direct result of an association between the two countries over nearly 300 years which had created certain loyalties, attitudes and aspirations. The basic facts in the political, economic and social development of Jamaica explain the reasons for this. First, Jamaica became a British territory in 1655 when it was captured from the Spaniards. Not only were all traces of Spanish occupation completely obliterated (but for the names of a few places) but also, since the Spanish occupation during the previous 250 years had resulted in the annihilation of the aborigines of the country (Arawak Indians), the British occupation of the island meant the beginning of a new society centred around slaves from Africa, absentee proprietors, attorneys, overseers, book-keepers and artisans from Britain, with the objective of sugar production for immediate profit.

Economically and numerically, the British people were in the dominant position during the earliest years of occupation. Although in 100 years the number of negro slaves had grown from 1,400 to 87,000, and the white population of 4,500 in 1658 had not quite doubled over the similar period, the dominant culture was that of the ruling class. There was complete disintegration of African culture. From the beginning the British established their legal system and over the years the judicial, political and social development followed the pattern known in England in the corresponding period.

Perhaps it was in the field of education that anglicizing was most evident. What young Jamaican did not sing lustily "Rule Britannia", or recite "Children of the Empire"? Who were the heroes of Jamaican children? Not Paul Bogle or William Gordon, but Nelson, Rodney, Clive of India and Gordon of Khartoum. The British poets were our poets. The British school examinations were our examinations, the schools in Jamaica were in so many instances run on identical lines and had similar curricula to those in England. Thus there were never any difficulties in transferring from one to the other. Yet some English people today are still amazed to know that Jamaicans' mother tongue is "English".

We sometimes hear in Britain all sorts of fears expressed about association and marriage between whites and blacks. This is not understood by Jamaicans because soon after the English occupation of the country, slave women began bearing children for white men of all social ranks, so that very early in the history of the island a coloured population was developing. These coloured people held a peculiar status in Jamaican society and from a situation of denial of political rights and limitations in property ownership, they became the purveyors of European culture from the eighteenth century onwards. Not only were they freed, but many were given schooling in England and by 1800 had outnumbered the whites.

Amongst this class it was seldom questioned that they should try to become as European as possible in appearance, speech, habits, thoughts and sympathy—a fact which has had a most profound effect upon the development of modern Jamaican society. The coloured class became the dominant class and it was inevitable in such circumstances that their values should become the ideals and objectives of the larger but less prosperous working class of predominantly black people. There was no room left for anything African. Instead, it was European values that began to be meaningful in the society.

The Role of the Christian Churches

Christianity has not been without significance in the emergence of these values. Attempts were at one time made to deny the slaves religion, but the churches won through. They did this largely on the basis of their teaching about the brotherhood of man and on their advocacy of the abolition of slavery. The churches were extensions of those originating in Britain—Anglican, Baptist, Methodist, Presbyterians, Moravians, Roman Catholics, Congregationalists, etc.

The traditional role of the Church in Jamaican society has remained. It has always meant association between British clergy and Jamaicans of every conceivable walk of life—an association which, whilst fulfilling the spiritual needs of the people, also helped in providing the experience (as has the presence of many other white people in Jamaica) of living and working together in an atmosphere of tolerance—which, alas, the Jamaican coming to Britain was to find less real and less sincere.

A Multi-Racial Society

The Jamaican society is a multi-racial society. There has been considerable intermixture amongst the various national groups. The population today comprises representatives of Negroes, British and other European peoples, Syrians, Jews, Indians, Chinese, as well as all possible mixtures. The society is truly multi-racial in that inter-group relationships are harmonious and there is a form of democracy which upholds equality of rights for all, rather than supports a situation in which an individual's ethnic origin confers the right to particularly advantageous or disadvantageous treatment. It is of some significance that when my country became an independent territory within the Commonwealth in 1962, Her Majesty the Queen sent a message which embodied the following:

> "It is with every good wish for the future that I warmly welcome Jamaica to the Commonwealth family of nations. I am sure that your country which has already given an example to the world of how people of many varied origins and traditions may live together in harmony, will have a vital contribution to make to the cause of further co-operation, understanding and tolerance far beyond the immediate area of the world in which it is situated."

None of this suggests that the Jamaican feels Britain owes him a livelihood or is begging for survival. It merely portrays a human situation in which inevitably certain types of expectations became cradled.

Despite the intense British cultural influence in the Caribbean we know that there are differences between the people of the West Indies and those of this country. But for colour, however, some of the differences are less sharp than those between the British and some other ethnic groups who have been settled here for many years. I believe that the world is all the more rich for the variety of cultures. What surprises the Jamaican is not so much the fact of being reminded that he is different, but the intense efforts of many to reject him completely on the basis that since his skin colour and hair-form are different this physical difference indicates a cultural difference to be abhorred.

The Immigrants' Expectations

Although many middle- and upper-class Jamaicans would, until our Independence in 1962, think of coming to Britain, as "going home", this is by no means an idea or ideal which has infected the majority of Jamaicans who have come to live and work here. In simple language, they have come out of sheer economic necessity and desire to fulfil their aspirations to achieve standards comparable with the best in any part of the world. This is their value system and this will always encourage them to move to any part of the world in which they think they can find this fulfilment.

They come with expectations of acceptance and tolerance—expectations cradled within the framework of the cultural and social experiences which I have described, and important enough to affect the immigrants' plans to come to Britain. Disappointment and dismay often come when these expectations are unfulfilled in Britain.

A useful division can be made here between expectations based on formal and informal teaching. The former category refers to the beliefs held about Britain which are passed on through formal sources. The Church and school have already been mentioned. Colonial Administration and Information Offices also contribute to these sources of knowledge which give rise to expectations.

Naturally, foremost among these hopes is that of improving one's economic position. The immigrants would certainly not come to Britain without the expectation of a job. A steady chance to work for much better rates of pay attracts the majority of immigrants. Together with this planned improvement in his work situation, the immigrant will expect a corresponding betterment in living conditions. A good wage should be able to purchase a reasonable place to live: a simple calculation which is often falsified when other factors are introduced.

The idea that Britain is a Christian country is widely held and carries certain implications for the prospective immigrant. He assures himself that however strange the conditions awaiting him, he will receive a welcome and a "reasonable" attitude from the majority of those he will meet. This idea that the *country* is Christian, must imply that the activities of small "anti" groups cannot be representative. The majority will be kind and welcoming regardless of troubles caused by a minority.

Beside this view, we can place the idea of British justice being fair. "Innocent until proven guilty" means a reasonable chance to gain admittance to the new society. These notions of fair play in a Christian society may not be assessable in the same way that job prospects are, but they are strongly believed by West Indians and disillusionment in this respect has a disturbing effect upon the whole of life for an immigrant. Of course, the Jamaican while still accepting that these principles guide official institutions like the Courts and the Church, has to contend with the general public and it is here he finds his real proving ground.

Another important point arises in relation to the knowledge of the West Indies which the immigrant expects to find in Britain. The formal sources of his knowledge of Britain, may lead the immigrant to expect a fair knowledge of his country from average Britons. The belief is often proved false and the result is disappointment and confusion.

The informal sources of the immigrant's expectations will depend on the norms and values of the society from which he comes. Because of the historical and social connections between Britain and the West Indies, a West Indian may well expect to

find important values and norms from his own society trans-
ferred to Britain. In many respects this is true. However, in
important instances the immigrant finds that other factors play
very important parts. An example will clarify. The channels of
upward mobility in West Indian society are linked with
economic advancement. For the most part, this is also true of
society in Britain. But the immigrant has to face the fact that
his colour is also taken into account much more than it used to
be. The fact that a man may keep the rules and yet be excluded
from the commensurate rewards, is an indication of special
status. The immigrant may find it hard to come to terms with
this special status and its implications.

The Church plays a very vigorous part in the life of the
smaller and less industrialized societies of the West Indies. The
Jamaican expects to find this extensive influence of the Church
in Britain's everyday life. In the busy industrial centres of
Britain life appears to be more fragmented and the Church
plays less of a central role, thus the immigrant may feel deprived
of an institution he can depend on.

He expects first of all to find that Church here means the
same as it does in his home country, and that Christianity is
based on the same principles throughout the world. To him in
many instances, the reception he gets as a stranger, the participation of the congregation, are not unlike the weather on a
cold and bleak February day. I have friends to whom it has
been suggested that they might be happier if they attended
another church—their faces did not fit. True enough the
Archbishop of Canterbury is Chairman of the National
Committee for Commonwealth Immigrants and there is
evidence of some churches making considerable effort to foster
better relationships between Commonwealth immigrants and
local people, but too often the Church *reflects* rather than
formulates opinion.

A Moral and Spiritual Issue
To the Jamaican his non-acceptance here is a moral issue. His
Church at home has always taken a strong stand on moral

issues, but in Britain he finds clergymen joining forces with
ethnocentric individuals rather than taking a strong stand on
issues which affect him. If an Englishman is glad to have a
Jamaican in church, why is he not glad to have him as his
neighbour, as his workmate, or his boss, if he is so qualified?
Is this Christianity? This trend undoubtedly shakes beliefs,
challenges convictions and leads to the inevitable conclusion
of having been hoodwinked.

Although the great majority of Jamaicans coming here were
members or adherents of one of the major denominations
at home, church attendance among the immigrants and participation in church life here is disappointingly low. Religious
leaders show concern but there seems to be no ready solution.
It is apparent that the Church in Britain—particularly in the
large industrial conurbations where the majority of immigrants
are—is less meaningful to British people than it was to these
Jamaicans at home, so that one has to look to other causes than
the indifference and apathy shown to immigrants, for paucity
of their attendance.

Is it that the newcomer is merely reflecting the *mores* of his
new environment? My own view is that no programme aimed
at getting more West Indians in church will succeed unless such
programmes can do something first about Church participation by natives of this country. It must be assumed that very
many of the reasons why they stay away must, in addition to
those peculiar to the immigrants, be applicable also. Certainly
the people from the Caribbean have been adjusting and adapting themselves to their new communities. The standards which
apply to those born here, the values which are inherent in the
society, are those to which acculturation takes place.

The Church must seek to teach honesty about race and race
relations. The Church must avoid double standards. It must not
look elsewhere for a mote when it has its own beams. When its
impact on the community is such that it becomes irresistible to
the majority, and when it can help society to function on the
basic principles of Christian beliefs, no one—not even a stranger
—can then successfully resist its leadership role in society.

PART III

By an African Student

Why Africans Come to Britain

Now that most peoples of Africa have attained independence there is a new awareness running through the whole continent. Development is the keynote and with it goes a feeling that Africans themselves must run their own affairs, whether in the Civil Service or in commerce and industry. This has resulted in a huge demand for trained personnel and has obliged African Governments and many private African students to use the educational facilities of the more developed nations. Britain has naturally received a large number of students from her former African colonies. What do these young men and women think of Britain and the British people and how are they treated in this country? I can only speak for myself but I think my experiences will be familiar to many other African students.

It is mainly the lack of adequate educational opportunities at home that brings Africans to this country. Many are doubtless ambitious and see the prospect of a fine career following on high academic qualifications; but they also understand clearly the importance of the role which they will have to play in the development of their countries.

Soon after we students have arrived in Britain we are prepared to give our verdict on the British people. This is that they are a reserved race, unconcerned with one another to a degree approaching unfriendliness. This quality appears to diminish as one gets away from London. But we cannot help noticing their co-operative spirit, hard work and helpfulness. Then, as we settle down, we begin to discover much more about the British people. The biggest shock we receive is in the field of Christianity.

Missionary Background

Being mostly Christian and having in many cases been educated in missionary schools with strong Christian influences we expect to find ourselves, as far as religious practice is concerned, at home in Britain. Britain is a country which is statistically almost wholly Christian and which Dr Billy Graham in his 1966 Greater London Crusade called the psychological leader of Christianity. From our superficial observation we find that Christianity is on the wane in this country.

Empty churches or churches half-full with the not-so-young are some of the manifestations of this visible decline in religious interest. Many British youths seem to give up their religious practices for fear of being ridiculed by their friends as old-fashioned or church fanatics. These facts often result in a decline in our own religious enthusiasm and even a total break-away from the Church. And when some of us finally fall away from the Christian flock no neighbouring Christian seems to notice and approach us with encouragement and help. The British appear to extend their attitude of minding one's own business to that of minding one's own soul. Even some Church ministers seem remote from their "sheep" and appear quite unapproachable, thus defeating the very purpose of their vocation.

The religious situation in Britain may not be as bad as some people make out but it is important to see how foreign students still look to this country for moral leadership. They find instead a selfish materialism. Africans, for whom Christianity is comparatively new, are particularly susceptible to this bad example. Did not the white man come from Britain to preach Christianity to us? Can the missionaries really have been sincere when this is all that Christianity means to the average Englishman? The thought strikes us that perhaps after all religion was just one more gun in the armoury of colonialism.

Need for Better Understanding

There are numerous Christian and other organizations in this country which assist overseas students by introducing them to British families, conducting tours to places of interest, arranging and conducting Bible studies, organizing social meetings and in various other ways. Through these bodies we soon begin to understand the British. It is then that we realize that the fast-moving, apparently unconcerned Englishman is quite a different person in his house. He is kinder, much less reserved and quite inquisitive. But we also discover that a good many Britons are amazingly ill-informed about our countries.

An Englishman once asked me how we were able to survive with wild animals roaming about everywhere in Africa. Such ignorance about other lands and subsequent misconceptions about their peoples often leads to prejudice. However, we are generally able to make quite good friends among the British people, although quietly disapproving parents will try to put an end to any boy-girl friendships. We also sense that the British have a preference for the simpler kind of African, someone who fits their conception of what an African should be like.

If Christians and other men of goodwill want to help us they will have to gain a better understanding of the problems we face, living in Britain. We get homesick in such a strange environment; few of us are able to marry here or have our families with us; all of us suffer from cold. We may have serious financial worries and studies, too, may get us down, conducted as they are in a language not our own. In matters of etiquette we may make mistakes, as although we have our own code of good manners (often very elaborate) they are not the same as in Britain.

Meeting Racial Discrimination

All this is difficult enough, but it is the common lot of all foreign students. They come here to learn and are prepared to put up with some discomforts. The African has often to deal with another and particularly unpleasant problem: racial discrimination. This shows itself especially in the field of accommodation. When we see notices saying "No Coloureds" or are told almost as much by landladies we are left in no doubt as to what some whites think of us. "Knock and the door shall be slammed in your face" is their policy with African students.

There are many other ways in which Britons show their colour-consciousness. We have noticed it in restaurants, dance-halls, trains, even, incredibly, in churches. Although perhaps slight, these displays of prejudice are deeply offensive to Africans who have at least their share of national and racial pride. Worse, they make us forget those many acts of kindness we experience from our British hosts.

Naturally, some Africans tolerate racial discrimination and prejudice better than others. Some react violently and carry back to their own countries bitter memories of their treatment in Britain. Many students go back to positions of power and responsibility and they may be tempted to "get their own back" on their white minorities. In this, just as in Christianity, Britain sets the example and has a heavy responsibility for what follows. If in addition to a degree the student returns home with a loathing of the white man and a contempt for "his" religion, a large part of the blame lies with the people of Britain. And not only in his own country but in the United Nations and other world organizations will the African voice these anti-white sentiments.

British Christians' Opportunity

It should be easy for the British people, and Christians in particular, to show us that they really want racial harmony. Here while they are our hosts they have every chance to demonstrate what they mean by "equality of man" and similar phrases. They are on their home ground.

In addition, a more positive attitude is looked for in Britons when they view the poisonous racialism in southern Africa. Some are quite unconcerned about this injustice and we cannot feel that such people are genuine in their dealings with us. And when they also profess themselves to be Christians we African Christians are dismayed and do not know what to think.

Provided we keep our common sense and are highly selective in the British ideas and attitudes that we absorb, there is a great deal that we can learn from our stay here. And at the very least I hope we will not be lacking in gratitude for being allowed to benefit from the excellent educational facilities in Britain.

CHAPTER ELEVEN

THE ROLE OF CHRISTIANS

by

Clifford S. Hill, M.A. (SOCIOLOGY), B.D.

The Reverend Clifford Hill is Director of
Research Studies in the Sociology of Religion
in the Congregational Church in England and
Wales, and Senior Lecturer in the Sociology of
Religion at the Barking Regional College of
Technology. For fifteen years he served as a
minister in charge of churches in areas of dense
immigrant settlement in London.

Missionary Activity

For the western churches the eighteenth and nineteenth centuries were characterized by a considerable amount of overseas missionary activity. Men felt impelled by the Holy Spirit to leave their comfortable European homes and to go to the so-called darker continents to "carry the glorious Gospel of the Blessed God" to those who had never heard of the name of Jesus. The evangelizing zeal of the church at this period knew no bounds, but alongside the missionaries there went others whose concern was commercial and imperialistic so that the white man's entry into areas where Europeans were hitherto unknown was not always directed towards the betterment and well-being of the local population. In spite of the handicap of the presence of some Europeans whose motives were anything but altruistic, the Church nevertheless successfully strove not only to preach the Gospel to all nations without regard to race or colour but also to meet the material needs and to minister to the physical well-being of the people. Mission hospitals and schools run by European churches were the first to bring medical care and education to people in many different parts of the world. Through the healing and teaching ministry of the Church large numbers were brought to Christ who might otherwise never have heard the Gospel.

The result of all this missionary activity was to create in the minds of many African, Asian and West Indian peoples an image of European Christians as having a real brotherly concern for them. This image, which had already become somewhat tarnished due to the activities of those Europeans who had gone overseas for purposes other than to preach, to teach and to heal, was further damaged by European resistance to the rising tide of national self-consciousness and the demands for independence that have characterized the twentieth-century development of many non-European peoples.

Immigration

By far the most damaging blow to the image of European Christendom has, however, been dealt by the large scale immigration of people from the tropical Commonwealth to Britain during the post-World-War II era. During this period many immigrants have arrived in Britain with high expectations in regard to living conditions and opportunities for employment in this country. Their unfulfilled hopes have resulted in disillusionment and despair—disillusionment with Britain and the British and the whole fabric of Commonwealth and her ties with the Mother Country.

For Christian immigrants the greatest disillusionment has been the dispelling of the image of "Christian Britain" by the cold reality of the situation they have seen with their own eyes. They have seen the widespread irreligiousness of life in Britain and the lack of any real evidence of welcome. But most of all their disillusionment has been occasioned not simply by the failure of the Christian Church to rise to their defence and officially champion their cause to secure justice and equality of treatment, but by the failure of the ordinary people in the churches to make them feel welcome and wanted when they attempt to worship God alongside their new white neighbours. These charges of being made to feel unwanted, so often repeated by Christians from Africa, from the West Indies and from Asia, surely represent the real indictment of the English churches. How many Christians brought to Christ by the labours of devoted Christians in the younger churches in their own lands have been lost to Christ by Christians in this country will never be known. One thing, however, is perfectly clear and that is that the very foundations of the Christian Church in many parts of the developing Commonwealth and even farther afield are being challenged today as never before, not by the resistance generated by other religious faiths or by internal strife and anti-Christian persecution, but by problems generated from Britain herself.

In the eyes of Christians from many parts of the

Commonwealth the evangelizing activities of British missionaries both today and in former generations are being invalidated
by the inability of the English churches to cope with immigration
problems. Disillusionment, loss of faith, and even the suspicion
that missionary activities were part of the imperialist plot to
subjugate non-European peoples, is not confined to those who
settle in Britain; these ideas quickly spread and have their
effects in the immigrants' homelands.

Thus we come face to face with both the heart and the vital
significance of the problem confronting the English churches.
It is this, that if the Church cannot translate into terms of
practical friendship and real dynamic love the Gospel of God's
Universal Fatherhood, her failure can have far-reaching
consequences. It could be a set-back to Christianity on a world-
scale for several generations to come.

Analysis of Failure

It may assist our thinking towards positive aims if at this
point we pause for a moment to examine the reasons for the
failure of the churches in this country to seize the initiative in
extending friendship and understanding to coloured immigrants
and students in Britain. When we speak of the failure of the
churches in this country as an accepted fact, demonstrably
true, we must not overlook the equally established fact of the
notable work done by certain churches and churchmen. Their
success in the field of race relations does not alleviate the
situation or exonerate those who have tried and failed or not
even tried. Indeed it serves to underline their indictment.

1. There has been a general failure on the part of Christians
in Britain to appreciate the extent, the significance or the
permanence of immigration from the new Commonwealth.
In this the Church has not been alone, she has been accompanied by politicians and planners, national and local
government officials, social workers and social agencies of
every kind.

In the late 1940's and early 1950's immigration was looked
upon as a temporary phenomenon; a mere post-war population

aberration that would settle down and sort itself out if left alone and provided nobody did or said anything. Despite the protests of local people and local papers in immigrant settlement areas this "head-in-the-sand" attitude of politicians and officials continued until the pipe-dream of peace and prosperity in booming Britain was abruptly shattered by the racial overtones and ugly violence of the 1958 Nottingham and Notting Hill riots.

Overnight there came the rude awakening for men who not only had refused to admit the existence of any social problems but who had also refused even to recognize the presence of the "strangers within our gate" and to accord them any kind of assistance in settlement or advice in personal problems or even the warmth of a friendly welcome. Suddenly churchmen and politicians were stirred into activity as they dashed to the microphone to disclaim responsibility for the dastardly deeds of the rioters and hurried off their press statements condemning all forms of racial intolerance. But the coloured immigrants were not deceived. Long before the riots erupted the rot had set in and they had already stepped out far on the road to disillusionment.

2. The Church, in common with secular institutions, both voluntary and official, was caught in a state of unpreparedness when at last the extent and permanence of Britain's rapidly growing coloured population was realized. In addition to the general tardy recognition of the situation that was developing, three other factors, in themselves unrelated, combined to militate against any effective preparation of the church to meet the task that now confronted her.

(a) The first of these factors is deeply rooted in the character-structure and general intransigence of outlook of the people of these islands. British insularity, whereby we have regarded from our island fortress the rest of the world as "foreigners" and ourselves as in some special way a favoured part of God's creation, destined to a role of world leadership but not to come into too close a contact with the lesser members of the human species, has led us to regard all those who do not emanate from these islands as in some way inferior to ourselves. The mild xenophobia with which we have for generations regarded all "foreigners" has been a constant source of irritation to others as well as a potentially dangerous factor in terms of a future day of reckoning when we would have to face realities about ourselves and the world of which we are *ipso facto* a part.

In spite of the Church's zeal for overseas missionary activity and in spite of Britain's far-flung Empire and vast overseas settlements, the majority of people in Britain knew little enough about the peoples, their customs or conditions of life in Africa, Asia or the Americas. Indeed the people of these isles knew very little about those who live just across the Channel and to whom they sweepingly referred as "continentals".

The effect of this insularity whereby we thought in terms of "us" and "the rest of the world" was not only to produce a very general and widespread ignorance of other peoples and cultures, but also to generate an attitude of superiority in regard to them. Thus when suddenly confronted with large numbers of people from the tropical Commonwealth settling in our midst the majority of people in the immigrant settlement areas of Britain, both churchgoers and non-churchgoers, reacted with their traditional shyness to foreigners bordering upon hostility. Even those who had an earnest desire to accord a welcome to the strangers found they knew so little about them that they did not possess the first idea as to how to set about welcoming them and making them feel at home.

(*b*) A second factor in the unpreparedness of the Church was that most of the immigrants settled (at least initially) in the poorer, densely populated, working-class areas of our large towns and cities where the churches were already facing considerable problems. Many of these churches were financially poorly supported and were saddled with large dilapidated buildings sadly in need of repair and modernization. Their ancillary buildings, halls and rooms, simply could not provide for the social needs of the community around them.

Many of these churches, moreover, lacked adequate lay leadership. The most able members of the community had moved out before the main wave of post-war immigration began and had settled in the more salubrious residential city suburbs. Their departure had left the churches in the inner city areas impoverished in a number of ways and thus unable to meet the new demands made upon them by the coming of immigrants from widely different parts of the world.

(c) The third factor contributing to the Church's lack of preparation to meet the demands of the situation created by large-scale immigration, concerns the settlement of Asians. Most of the immigrants from India and Pakistan belong to non-Christian religions. A great majority of them are Hindus and Moslems, many of them being sincere and devout in their religious beliefs. For the Christian Church in this country this was the mountain coming to Mohammet; a reversal of the role whereby for generations the English-speaking churches have sent missionaries to the Indian sub-continent.

But the Christian "missionaries" in this country were not prepared when the people came to them. For one thing the situation was complicated by difficulties in communication. Less than 20 per cent. of new arrivals from India and Pakistan have an adequate knowledge of the English language. The resultant problem of communication has affected all social institutions. Employment officers, personnel managers in industry, doctors and social workers have all been faced with the same difficulty in understanding and meeting the needs of the newcomers. Ministers, priests and congregations in the areas of Asian immigrant settlement for the most part regarded the newcomers as presenting a problem quite beyond their capacity to help. With a few isolated exceptions little or nothing was done by the Church to meet either the religious or the social implications of the situation.

3. The third and final major factor that we shall look at in our brief analysis of the reasons for the Church's failure to seize the initiative and meet the demands of the situation created by immigration concerns the social problems and

physical environment of the immigrant settlement areas. The fact that the immigrants settled in the highly industrialized urban areas of Britain is well known, but what is not always appreciated is that most of these areas already contained complex social problems *before* the coming of coloured people. They were the overcrowded, depressed working-class areas already well on the way to becoming slums with a poor standard of housing, many families living under grossly overcrowded conditions, suffering from racketeer landlords and faced with all attendant evils and vice that such areas naturally generate.

The churches in these areas were already faced with grave problems. With the rapid influx of large numbers of coloured immigrants from widely different national and cultural backgrounds, the problems of evangelism and of offering adequate pastoral service assumed mammoth proportions. Most of the immigrants and many of the local white people were living in furnished rooms and thus lacked any real security of tenure. This produced a highly mobile population that further complicated any attempts at settled pastoral work. The clergy found they could not keep pace with the movements of their people from one address to another and because of this large numbers became "lost" to the Church.

Many of the churches in these areas, moreover, lacked specialist-trained men and women to tackle the social, psychological and religious problems presented by such a complex admixture of population. Many of the clergy struggled on manfully with the hopeless task but were often baffled and discouraged by the lack of response of the immigrants and by their own inability to do more than scratch the surface of the situation they saw all around them. This lack of response on the part of the immigrants often stemmed from the feeling of not being fully understood by the host population, either professional or lay, due to their different backgrounds, but it was also partly due to the "culture shock" to which most immigrants are subjected upon arrival in Britain. This culture shock is a psychological effect due to the adjustment required by the difference between the expectations and anticipations of the immigrant and the reality he finds in experience.

Needs and Opportunities

1. There is clearly a need for more research to be carried out in the immigrant settlement areas to discover the real feelings, reactions and needs of the immigrants. In this connection it would be useful if there were much closer liaison between the churches of different denominations in pooling their experiences for the benefit of all those who have the real welfare of the immigrants at heart.

2. There needs to be more efficient use made of the Church's available man-power. Men and women who have worked overseas in those part of the Commonwealth from which the immigrants emanate ought to be encouraged to give at least a period of service to the Church in one of the immigrant settlement areas. Such a policy could be of the greatest significance in the areas of Asian settlement. Where the Church can approach Indians and Pakistanis not merely with the dumb hand of friendship but with the Gospel of Love spoken in their own language, the work of the Church in bringing all nations to Christ could be much more effective.

3. The use of men who have worked in the West Indies could be a great asset to the churches in areas of West Indian settlement in helping both clergy and lay workers to understand the background of the immigrants. This is particularly essential in regard to their family and matrimonial traditions as well as their social and religious customs.

4. Men with first-hand knowledge of the West Indies could also help to create that climate of goodwill within the local church congregations that is so essential if the immigrants are to be accepted within the church. It is not sufficient for the clergy and church officials to tell them they are welcome. It is necessary for them to "feel" that welcome within the congregation and to see it translated into terms of practical friendship among the ordinary Christians in the congregation.

5. The Church needs to develop new techniques of using the existing bridgeheads with the immigrant community and developing and building upon such ready-made contacts as she already has with members of the immigrant communities. In regard to Christian immigrants, baptisms, weddings and the regular or even occasional practice of their religious observances, provide natural bridgeheads. There are others, such as the immigrants' need for social intercourse within their own communities. Due to their overcrowded living conditions they need the provision of halls or rooms where they can meet or entertain their friends. This provides an opportunity for the Church to contact as well as to serve the immigrants.

6. What is needed above all is a wider vision of the whole sphere of inter-racial relationships. If the situation in Britain is to be redeemed, or the separation between white and coloured in South Africa is to be broken, or the hostility between Negro and white in the U.S.A. (intensified by the riots of the hot summer of 1967) is to be countered, each local situation must be seen in the context of the whole world situation.

The race problem is a world issue. In the context of the nuclear age it presents the greatest threat to the peace of the world and to the future existence of mankind in history. Such a threat can only be effectively countered by a world-wide movement of reconciliation. No secular philosophy can accomplish this mammoth task of remoulding the minds of men. Among world religions only Christianity can provide the breadth of vision and the spiritual power to accomplish this.

In spite of past or present failures the Christian Church, with its gospel of salvation firmly based in the Universal Fatherhood of God together with its world-wide outreach, provides the one real hope for achieving inter-racial peace. This objective will not be accomplished by the pronouncements of committees, the findings of working parties, or even by the faithful labours of missionaries and preachers. Peace on a world scale between men of all races and colours can only be achieved by Christians of all nations being fully committed to the "ministry of reconciliation". Such is the size of the task. The challenge is enormous, but the consequences of failure are unthinkable.

The role of the Church in the immigrant settlement areas of Britain is highly significant and of great importance for the future of race relations in this country from both a sociological and a religious standpoint. In the context of the Church's role in society it is important for coloured people to be admitted into the community of Christian congregations and to participate in parish and church fellowship activities on terms of absolute equality with their white neighbours. Such participation within the church, as one of the major social institutions, reflects a degree of integration within a section of the community that can provide a matrix for the whole of society. If the most able immigrants are given positions within the church commensurate with their abilities and are seen thus to be making a contribution to the life of the church, this has the effect of raising the status of the whole immigrant community in the eyes of the white members of the congregation.

Religious Apartheid

The factor that is all important here is that when coloured immigrants participate fully in the activities of the local church they are participating in an English institution, the coloured man is thus making a contribution to the host society. Conversely the danger exists that where immigrants of ability feel unwelcome within the church and find their talents are not called into service they will remain outside the English churches and form their own religious associations catering either largely or exclusively for coloured people. This is not a hypothetical reaction to a hypothetical sense of rejection, but a statement of what has already happened and is still happening on an increasing scale. The mushroom growth of the numerous little West Indian Pentecostal congregations since the early 1960's is evidence of this fact. The leaders of these immigrant churches usually claim to have tried to worship within English churches but to have experienced rejection in one form or another. The most significant part of this movement is the number of adherents of these immigrant churches who had no previous Pentecostal background before coming to Britain.

In the West Indies, Pentecostals represent only about 5 per cent. of the total Christian community. No reliable figures for church attendance of West Indian immigrants in Britain are available, but in 1967 it was estimated that at least 50 per cent. of West Indian immigrants who were regular churchgoers attended churches run by and mainly or exclusively attended by coloured people. By no means all of these immigrant churches are Pentecostal. Many of them are run on traditional Free Church lines; some even claim to be Episcopal. Many of those who attend these churches and religious groups formerly were members of one of the major denominations, Catholic, Anglican, or Free Church.

The real danger of this movement is not merely that it represents a measure of religious apartheid which in itself could have serious consequences in the future, especially if the children of immigrants continue to adhere to these all-coloured congregations, but that the growth of this movement reflects the measure of the failure of the English churches. If the churches in Britain cannot gather within their fold West Indian Christians who were practicing adherents of these same churches in their homelands, they will have failed not only to provide a ground for integration into a section of the community which could provide a valuable stepping stone for integration into the wider community, but their failure will have wider implications. It will mean that the churches in this country have failed on their own ground to meet the basic spiritual needs of the immigrants and failed moreover to provide the friendship and love which is basic to their Gospel and which they exist to proclaim to the world. Thus the Church's task in regard to gathering the immigrants within its fold has real religious significance. Her failure in so vital a sphere that touches upon the heart of her witness, and the basic tenets of the Fatherhood of God and the brotherhood of man for which she stands, can lead to a measure of discrediting which could prove a serious set-back to her mission, not merely in Britain, but in many other parts of the world.

The Church Holds the Key

A further implication of this situation is that the Church as the representative body of Christian opinion has traditionally been looked upon as the formulator of public opinion on vital questions touching the basic moral principles which are the foundations of our democracy. If the Church were discredited in the matter of receiving immigrants and integrating them into her own membership in this country this could have a serious effect upon the Church's role as the formulator of opinion on such issues.

Thus the churches in Britain are faced both with an unparalleled challenge and opportunity. Their failure as well as their success could have immense significance in the future days. Christians have the opportunity of doing two things of great importance for the future of race relations in this country which in turn could have even wider significance in the world. In the first place they have the opportunity of providing within the Christian Church a matrix of the new society where white and coloured are bonded together by love and mutual respect and engage in objective-based co-operative activities. Secondly, Christians, in the confidence derived from the knowledge of their own success in this field, can act as the formulators of opinion within the wider community; the leaven within the lump. This is a vital role for Christians to fulfil for it may be fairly doubted whether any other body or group within society has the necessary moral precepts strong enough to fulfil this role.

The Christian attitude to race is based upon a doctrine of man that stems directly from its concept of man's place within a theologically conceived universe. Without such a monotheistic concept of the universe centred in a Divine Universal Fatherhood which implies a brother and sister relationship for the whole of mankind without regard to race, nation or colour, there could be no universal command laid upon man to act towards his fellow man in brotherly love. Holding such a doctrine, Christians cannot remain true to their beliefs and to their claim to be followers of Christ without taking to their hearts their brethren of another colour. For Christians the commandment of Christ is absolute, "This is my commandment, that you love one another as I have loved you" (John xv. 12).

BIBLIOGRAPHY

Chapter I—Introductory

HAZELDEN, KYLE, *The Racial Problem in Christian Perspective* (London), Lutterworth 1960.

HILL, CLIFFORD S., *How Colour Prejudiced is Britain?* (London), Panther 1967.

MASON, PHILIP, *Common Sense about Race* (London), Gollancz 1961.

P. E. P. REPORT (London), Penguin 1967.

RICHMOND, ANTHONY H., *The Colour Problem* (London), Penguin 1961.

Chapter II—Migration in the World Setting

BORRIE, W. D., *The Cultural Integration of Immigrants* (Paris), Unesco 1959.

DE CHARDIN, TEILHARD, *Le Milieu Divin* (Paris), Editions du Seuil 1957; (translated from the French by Bernard Wall and others) (London), Collins 1960.

KELSEY, GEORGE D., *Racism and the Christian Understanding of Man* (New York), Scribner 1965.

KENNEDY, JOHN FITZGERALD, *A Nation of Immigrants* (rev. and enl. edition) (London), Hamish Hamilton 1964.

LIND, ANDREW W. (ed), *Race Relations in World Perspective.* Papers read at the Conference on Race Relations in World Perspective (Honolulu), University of Hawaii Press, 1954.

SEGAL, RONALD, *The Race War* (London), Jonathan Cape 1966.

UNESCO, *The Positive Contribution by Immigrants* (Paris), Unesco 1955.

WILSON, FRANCESCA M., *They Came as Strangers* (London), Hamish Hamilton 1959.

WORLD POPULATION CONFERENCE, Rome, August–September 1954, Proceedings: papers, Vol. 2 (New York), United Nations 1956.

Chapter III—The Rights of Individuals and Duties of States

FREUDENBERG, A., *Is there a Christian Right of Migration?* (Geneva), mimeographed report of the W.C.C., Leysin Conference 1961.

INTERNATIONAL CATHOLIC MIGRATION COMMISSION, *Anthology of Papal Documents on Migration* (Geneva), I.C.M.C. 1965.

LAUTERPACHT, H., *International Law and Human Rights* (London), Stevens 1950.

STARK, TADEUSZ, *Liberté de Migration* (The Hague), "PAX" International Publishing Co., Ltd., 1954.

UNITED NATIONS, *Study of Discrimination in Respect of the Right of Everyone to Leave Any Country* (New York), United Nations 1963.

WILLIAMS, COLIN W., *Does a Nation-State have the Right to Restrict Immigration?* (Geneva), report of the W.C.C., Leysin Conference 1961.

Chapter IV—Racial Images and Attitudes in Britain—The Background

BANTON, MICHAEL (ed), *Darwinism and the Study of Society* (London), Tavistock 1961.

— *Race Relations* (London), Tavistock 1967.

FOOT, PAUL, *Immigration and Race in British Politics* (London), Penguin 1965.

HUXLEY, ELSPETH, *Back Street New Worlds* (London), Chatto & Windus 1964.

LITTLE, KENNETH, *Negroes in Britain* (London), Routledge & Kegan Paul 1947.

PATTERSON, SHEILA, *Dark Strangers* (London), Tavistock 1963.

Chapter V—The Psychology of Prejudice

ADORNO, T. W., *The Authoritarian Personality* (New York), Harper 1950.

ALLPORT, GORDON W., *The Nature of Prejudice* (Boston), Beacon Press 1954.

GARN, STANLEY M. (ed), *Readings on Race* (Oxford), Blackwells Scientific Publications 1960.

MEDAWAR, P. B., *The Future of Man* (London), Methuen 1960.
NIEBUHR, REINHOLD, *The Children of Light and the Children of Darkness* (New York), Scribner 1944.
SIMPSON, G. and YINGER, JOHN, *Racial and Cultural Minorities* (New York), Harper & Row 1953.
TINBERGEN, NIKO, *The Herring Gull's World* (London), Collins 1953.
YOUNG, KIMBALL, *Handbook of Social Psychology* (2nd ed rev) (London), Routledge & Kegan Paul 1957.

Chapter VI—The Biology of Race
DOBZHANSKY, T., *Mankind Evolving* (New Haven and London), Yale University Press 1962.
DUNN, L. C., *Heredity and Evolution in Human Populations* (London), O.U.P. 1959.
GARN, S. M., *Human Races* (2nd ed) (Springfield, Illinois), Charles C. Thomas 1966.
HARRISON, G. A., WEINER, J. S., TANNER, J. M. and BARNICOT, N. A., *Human Biology* (Oxford), Clarendon Press 1964.
HOWELLS, W. W., *Mankind in the Making* (London) Secker & Warburg 1960.
MATHER, K., *Human Diversity* (Edinburgh and London), Oliver & Boyd 1964.

Chapter VII—The Christian View of Intermarriage
GRAY, A. HERBERT, *Men, Women and Gods* (London), S.C.M. 1943 (rev. ed).
JABAVU, NONI, *Drawn in Colour* (London), John Murray 1960.
MEAD, MARGARET, *Male and Female* (London), Gollancz 1950.
MÜLLER-LYER, F., *The Evolution of Modern Marriage—A Sociology of Sexual Relations* (London), Allen & Unwin 1930
UWEMEDIMO, ROSEMARY, *Mammy-wagon Marriage* (London), Hurst & Blackett 1961.

Chapter VIII—The Biblical Doctrine of Race
BOYD, MALCOLM (ed), *On the Battle Lines* (London), S.C.M. 1965.

KERKBOEK HANDEL, N. G., *Delayed Action: An Ecumenical Witness from the Afrikaans Speaking Church*, available from P.O. Box 245 Pretoria.

PRICE, T., *Christianity and Race Relations* (London), S.C.M. 1954.

SELBIE, W. B., *The Fatherhood of God* (London), Duckworth 1936.

SMITH, C. RYDER, *The Bible Doctrine of Man* (London), Epworth 1951.

TAYLOR, J. V., *Christianity and Politics in Africa* (London), Penguin 1957.

Chapter IX—The Theology of Race

CONGAR, Y., *The Catholic Church and the Race Question* (Paris), Unesco 1953.

— *Ecumenical Statements on Race Relations* (Geneva), World Council of Churches 1965.

TAVARD, GEORGE, *Vatican II and the Race Question:* Continuum, Spring 1966, pp. 129–37.

VISSER'T HOOFT, W. A., *The Ecumenical Movement and the Racial Problem* (Paris), Unesco 1954.

Chapter X—A Look at Britain

BRITISH COUNCIL, *How to Live in Britain: a handbook for students from overseas* (London), Longmans 1962.

CLARKE, EDITH, *My Mother Who Fathered Me* (London), Allen & Unwin 1957.

CURTIN, P. DE A., *The Image of Africa* (London), Macmillan 1965.

DAVIDSON, B., *Which Way Africa?—The Search for a New Society* (London), Penguin 1964.

DESA, RASHMI, *Indian Immigrants in Britain* (London), O.U.P. 1963.

HENRIQUES, FERNANDO, *Family and Colour in Jamaica* (London), Eyre & Spottiswood 1953.

— *Jamaica, Land of Wood and Water* (London), McGibbon 1957.

LAMB, B. P., *India: A World in Transition* (London), Pall Mall 1963.

MARRIOTT, McKIM (ed), *Village India: Studies in the Little Community* (London), O.U.P. 1955.

RUBIN, VERA (ed), *Caribbean Studies: A Symposium* (Nottingham), Hall 1960.

Chapter XI—The Role of Christians

CALLEY, M. J. C., *God's People—West Indian Sects in England* (London), Oxford 1965.

CHURCH ASSEMBLY, Board For Social Responsibility, *Together in Britain: A Christian Handbook on Race Relations* (London), Church Information Office 1960.

DE JONG, P., *Migration and the Christian Faith* (The Hague), The Research Group for European Migration Problems 1964.

HILL, C. S., *West Indian Migrants and the London Churches* (London) Oxford 1963.

SECRETARIAT FOR MIGRATION, *Migration Today—Current Problems and Christian Responsibility* (Geneva), W.C.C. (twice yearly).

WORLD COUNCIL OF CHURCHES, Secretariat for Migration, *Within Thy Gates:* The Report on the Conference on migrant workers in Western Europe, held at Arnoldshain in 1963 (Geneva), W.C.C. 1964.